D1560925

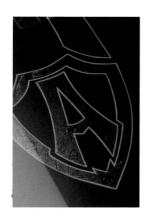

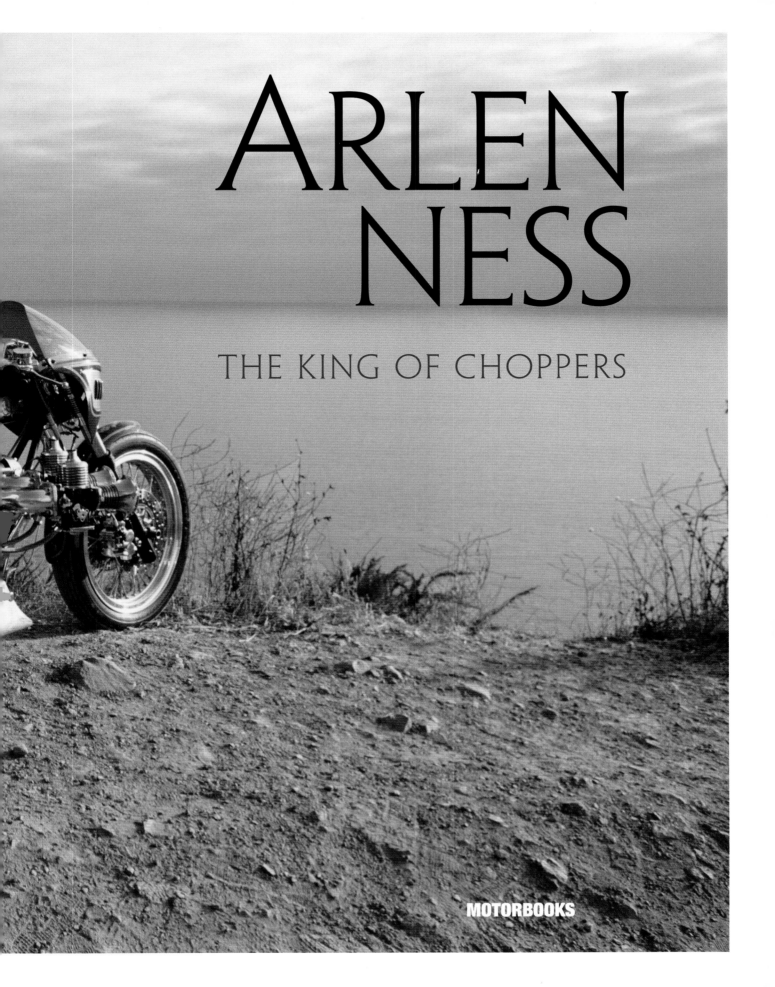

ARLEN NESS

THE KING OF CHOPPERS

MOTORBOOKS

IN MEMORY OF ELAINE AND
ERVIN NESS, LARRY KUMFERMAN, AND
JIM DAVIS. WHILE THEY ARE NOT
HERE TO SHARE IN ARLEN'S SUCCESS,
THEY WERE BEHIND SO MANY
OF THESE BIKES AND SO MUCH OF THIS
STORY. THEY WOULD BE VERY PROUD.

First published in 2005 by Motorbooks, an imprint
of MBI Publishing Company, Galtier Plaza, Suite 200,
380 Jackson Street, St. Paul, MN 55101-3885 USA

The information in this book is true and complete to the
best of our knowledge. All recommendations are
made without any guarantee on the part of the author or
Publisher, who also disclaim any liability incurred in
connection with the use of this data or specific details.

We recognize that some words, model names, and
designations mentioned herein are the property of
the trademark holder. We use them for identification
purposes only.

Motorbooks titles are also available at discounts in bulk
quantity for industrial or sales-promotional use. For details
write to Special Sales Manager at MBI Publishing
Company, Galtier Plaza, Suite 200, 380 Jackson Street,
St. Paul, MN 55101-3885 USA.

ISBN 0-7603-2219-8

Editor: Darwin Holmstrom
Designer: Rochelle Schultz

Printed in China

On the cover: Arlen Ness aboard *Top Banana,* the bike
with which he won Discovery Channel's *Biker Build-Off.*

On the frontispiece: Arlen and family pose on *Top Banana*
at the completion party. Left to right: Bev, Arlen, Cory,
Kim, Zach, Sherri, and Craig. Seated on floor: Max, Taylor,
and Samantha, 2005.

On the title page: Arlen riding his *Blower Bike,* 1987.

On the back cover: Arlen fitting lines on *Top Banana,*
Dublin, California, 2004.

CONTENTS

Sonny Barger in Sturgis,
South Dakota, 2004.

FOREWORD

I FIRST met Arlen back in the mid-1960s, when he still had his day job but was spending most of his nights in a garage in Hayward, putting flame designs and metal-flake paint on peanut gas tanks. Then he started doing frames, fenders, and other custom-machined and chromed parts. We had a lot in common. We both lived in East Oakland, had started out riding Cushman scooters while in our early teens, then graduated to used Harleys. When we began customizing our bikes back then, none of us imagined they would eventually be considered worthy of being displayed in museums as artistic achievement—we were just having fun and trying to create something different, faster, and cooler. Taking the fenders off and replacing the handlebars of the stock bikes was considered heresy by some of the Harley-Davidson dealers who banned us from their shops and wouldn't even sell parts to us.

A few years later Arlen opened his own parts store on East 14th Street in Oakland, where there used to be a dirt bike shop. By that time custom bikes were becoming much more popular, and Arlen was starting to be recognized as one of the premier innovators. He never compromised on his vision of what bikes could look like and wasn't dissuaded by those who considered him too offbeat. The last bike I built for my wife Sharon in 1996 was mostly with parts from his shop.

Arlen is just a year younger than me, and one thing we have in common is neither of us expected to be around this many years. But even through hard times, we are both fortunate to still be doing what we enjoy most. When Arlen's business grew prosperous enough that someone suggested he close the store and just do mail order, I know he refused. He said, "The people who come to the store are the people who put us in business." I think that about says it all about Arlen: he never forgot where he started!

Sonny Barger
Phoenix, Arizona
March 2005

Arlen rides up the ramp to the second story of his
new store, Dublin, California, 2003.

ACKNOWLEDGMENTS

I WOULD like to thank the many people, some of whom I have known for over 20 years and others that I met over the course of this project. They generously offered their time to recount their experiences of the early years with Arlen and of custom biking. Arlen's wife, Bev, and children, Cory and Sherri, took time from their personal lives and Arlen Ness, Inc., in which they are so active, to talk with me extensively. To go back to the 1960s, brother-in-law Rich Rego, who was there on his own Knucklehead, and Arlen's brother, Kevin, who was helping out in the garage, were very helpful. Harry Brown shared paint techniques with Arlen and his earliest biking memories with me. Since so little has been written about these times, I could not have compiled this story without the collective memories of Steve Allington, Arnie Araujo, Keith Ball, Gary Bang, Carl Brouhard, Charlie Bryant, Barry Cooney, Dick DeBenedictis, Bob Dron, David Edwards, Arlin Fatland, Danny Gray, Ultan Guilfoyle, Larry Hoppe, Horst, Matt Hotch, Billy Lane, John "Pretty Boy" Lopez, Jack Luna, Jeff McCann, Bob "Mun" Munroe, Dave Nichols, Nick Nichols, Dave Perewitz, Susan Perewitz, Grady Pfeiffer, Perry Sands, Bruce Siegal, Donnie Smith, Dan Stern, Joe Teresi, and Paul Yaffe.

Darwin Holmstrom, my editor on this, my fourth book with Motorbooks, has once again offered me the encouragement to keep my fingertips jumping across the keyboard when they may have felt they deserved a break. His agility at reworking awkward phrases or finding a word that was beyond my reach may have readers of this book believing I could be a writer after all. His coworker Rochelle Schultz in the art department has again worked her magic with the layout, type and design. She makes us all look good.

Without Steve Temple and Emily Marshall, who I work with daily and who have put so many days into this project, we could never have gone to press. A special thank you to Catherine and my children, Sean and Kiera, who make every effort to tolerate my countless hours and late nights since I get so involved with these projects. I could not have written this without them. Most of all, I want to thank Arlen himself. He gave me weeks of his time to help make this happen. Since the day we met years ago, he has been generous of himself in every conceivable way. He is a friend.

Michael Lichter

INTRODUCTION

THIS book celebrates the life, career, and art of Arlen Ness. His story is best told through the custom motorcycles he builds. Every artist's work tells of that artist's life experiences, and in many ways these motorcycles are like rolling sculptures that have captured Arlen's history.

Despite having photographed a number of Arlen's bikes in the past, I decided early in this project to re-shoot them in the studio so all the bikes would appear in the same style, stripped of any distraction. The goal: to encourage the reader to focus on what is most important—the bikes themselves. A project like this would not have been possible with any other builder. No one else has had as prolific a career, nor has anyone been able to keep the sheer quantity of bikes Arlen has kept (or bought back).

For almost 40 years, Arlen has been a trendsetter, quietly and steadily producing some of the most creative custom bikes the world has ever seen. He was the first to try many innovative ideas, and on numerous occasions his designs evolved into popular styles, setting the trend for custom bikes to come. Year after year, even when custom bike building was going through hard times, he came out with spectacular new machines that caught the attention of the media and riding public. He ascended to the top of this billion-dollar industry at a time when you could hardly call it an industry at all, and he has remained at the top ever since.

It would be appropriate if I had met Arlen on an assignment photographing one of his custom bikes, but actually we met at a barbecue in the Harley Heaven pit area of the Daytona Speedway. It was 1982, and I was covering bike week for *Easyriders* magazine. Arlen and I just happened to be standing next to each other in line. What a great way to meet: informally. With his quiet and unassuming nature, it took me a few minutes to realize that he was *the* Arlen Ness, well known by me and everyone else who was into bikes at that time. I was in awe.

In the years that followed, our paths would cross each year at events like Sturgis and Daytona. There were also occasions when I was assigned to shoot one of his new bikes. I ran into him on the slopes at Winter Park, Colorado, the year after we first met. He was with his old friend Arlin Fatland, owner

Arlen and family on the deck of the Castro Valley house. Left to right: Bev, Arlen, Kim, Cory, and Sherri, 1987.

of 2-Wheelers in Denver, while I happened to be visiting family. This was one of the only times either Arlen or Arlin had ever been on skis. We met for a drink later in the day, before they had to head out of town. While the three of us visited, a buzz went through the bar. An avalanche had closed the mountain pass back to Denver. A mad scramble to the pay phones ensued, but there were no vacancies to be had. There was, however, room on our couches for both of them.

Arlen and I met on other occasions, like when we spent a day up in Banff, Canada. We went up to Lake Louise after a bomb went off at the Calgary bike show we were supposed to attend and the show was cancelled. On another occasion, I spent several days at Arlen and Bev's Manter Street house working on a story on him for a German business magazine.

I'm starting to sound like the many people interviewed for this book with story after story to tell. For friends and family to talk about Arlen is to relive the many fun experiences that they shared. He never seems too busy (although now I realize how busy he really is) to make time. Whether it's someone

stopping to ask for an autograph or a friend in need, he makes himself available.

Most of Arlen's closest friends ride. Many are big industry players, some are serious garage builders, while others are just riding enthusiasts. All these friends and, for that matter, everyone who knows Arlen respects him for his achievements and for who he is as a person, both of which are always described using superlatives. This respect is how Arlen came to deserve the title "King of Choppers."

Admittedly, the term *chopper* is used as a loose definition rather than specifically referring to a style of custom bike with a long, raked front end. Arlen has chopped his share of bikes, starting with his first Knuckle in 1963, and he still chops them today, but along the way he's explored every type of custom bike that he, or anyone for that matter, could imagine.

Arlen has earned the title "King." He's the benchmark against which other builders are measured. He's the one who helped turn custom bike building into an industry. He's the one to whom young builders go to pay respect, ask for advice, and for

Cory, Arlen, and Bev at Arlen and Bev's house for a family gathering, Alamo, California, 2003.

encouragement. As custom-bike builder Matt Hotch said after unexpectedly dropping in to visit Arlen while filming a *Biker Build-Off* in Northern California: "Arlen takes care of everyone. Even though everyone else is his competition, he doesn't look at it that way. He is very selfless. That's a hard quality to find in people."

As I was gathering material for this book, it was clear that readers would be interested in Arlen's early motorcycle experiences. The 1960s were a period when the seeds of today's custom motorcycle industry were just being planted and its roots starting to take hold, yet so little was chronicled. Arlen, and many of his friends, was too busy working and having fun to worry about writing things down or committing experiences to memory. Besides, these were the years when a fifth of tequila didn't last long and memories merged together. It was a time for Arlen when the invincibility and excitement of youth melded with enthusiasm for the future. There was anticipation of a world ahead where anything was possible.

After piecing this story together from many sources, Arlen may not have changed as much as I thought at first. More than 40 years after buying his first Knuckle, he is still busy working, having fun, and operating in a world where anything is possible. In his sixties now, he is as excited and turned on building custom bikes as he was in his twenties. With his son Cory as president of Arlen Ness, Inc., where he is responsible for the daily running of the business and his daughter Sherri heading up public relations, human resources, and many other details, Arlen may be having more fun than ever. His latest creation, *Top Banana*, which he fabricated for a Discovery Channel *Biker Build-Off,* is as creative as his earliest big-project bikes, like *Untouchable* and *Two Bad*. As for retiring, Arlen would have to consider what he does every day "work" to be able to do that. To stop creating and doing something that he loves so much, I don't believe that's in Arlen's future.

Arlen in his new
Lamborghini Diablo,
Dublin, California, 2004.

MODEL FOR SUCCESS

View of the new showroom, retail area, and glassed-in museum from Arlen's office, Dublin, California, 2004.

FROM a glass-walled second-floor office in the 70,000-square-foot headquarters building of Arlen Ness Enterprises, Inc., Arlen Ness looks over the rewards of 35 years of hard work, the result of slowly and steadily building a custom motorcycle dynasty.

Down below, over 100 bikes are for sale on the showroom floor. Some in-house customs bear his name, as do the Ness Signature Series Vegas and Kingpin models that Arlen and his son, Cory, helped design for Victory Motorcycles. The bulk of the bikes are the production bikes that have become so popular over the last few years. American Ironhorse and Big Dog are well represented with their long front ends and wild paint jobs, no two alike. There are also more conservative Victorys and even a few Vespa scooters for the curious who aren't quite ready for a big twin. On one side of the showroom floor is a huge parts department full of Ness product, while on the other side is a retail area chock full of apparel, games, and accessories, all bearing Arlen's very recognizable "A" trade-

mark. If Arlen wants, he can watch the busy group of telephone salespeople to get a pulse on business activity, or he can look across at the 4,000-square-foot museum that houses over 50 of his custom creations. More often than not, Arlen's office sits empty because he's too busy creating custom bikes, working hard in the shop, or traveling across the country and around the globe to waste time sitting around contemplating how he rose to the pinnacle of the motorcycle world.

Arlen rarely reflects on his own success, success he never planned for. That's one of his unique traits; he has never planned too far ahead. Life came and went one fabricated part at a time. He laid out goals that were clear, short-term, and attainable. In part, this is because what he has achieved had never been done before; it had never even been dreamt of. There were no models for success in the custom motorcycle business when Arlen started out. Today, thousands of custom bike shops sell choppers, there are numerous 300-page parts catalogs from which you can bolt together a custom bike, and almost any night of the week, you can tune into the Discovery Channel and see cable-made motorcycle celebrities and a new model for success.

Before there was a custom bike industry, every custom part had to be hand fabricated. In small garages across America, bikers cut, bent, and welded metal to build their own bikes. They may have painted the bikes themselves, too. Arlen worked like this. He learned as he went along, doing it all himself. Eventually he recognized his own shortcomings and knew that if he were to achieve something as outstanding as he envisioned, he would have to enlist outside help.

When his business was still small, he came up with the tag line "Quality Motorcycle Parts from California Craftsmen." Whether a bike was being displayed at a show or featured in a motorcycle magazine, contributors were clearly identified and thanked. Arlen's fellow craftsmen appreciated the credit, as well as Arlen's sense of honesty, fairness, and respect. Their response was to strive for perfection, producing the highest quality work possible. Arlen's manner, his team, and the bikes he built became his formula for success. One bike at a time, one bike after another, his recognition from show spectators, from the industry, and from the motorcycle press grew to what it is now, with Arlen being one of the most esteemed and accomplished custom motorcycle builders in the world.

Arlen is a little older and has been riding bikes a lot longer than most custom motorcycle riders of today. These younger riders may be aware that Arlen is considered

a legend, but they probably don't know many of the bikes that made him famous. It's even less likely that they know where Arlen came from or the world in which he grew up. To understand these things is to better understand Arlen.

America had come out of the Depression and was preparing for war by the time Arlen was born to working-class parents in 1939. While he was still an infant, his family moved from Minnesota to California, where he and his mother, Elaine, lived. Arlen's dad, Ervin, fought in the European Theater in World War II. After being injured, his dad returned home and was offered a job in Iowa, where the young family then moved. Two years later, brighter prospects brought them back to Northern California, where Ervin took a job delivering furniture, and they finally settled in Oakland. Elaine also worked, taking a part-time job at a dry cleaners, which allowed the couple to start saving money.

For entertainment, Arlen's parents both bowled, sometimes in two or three leagues a week. Arlen would go with them and just hang out or play pinball. In his free time, he also played a lot of sports. Baseball kept him occupied all summer, but he gave it up after

Arlen bowling in Castro Valley, California, 1987.

Lifetime achievement "Vicky" award from *V-Twin* magazine, 2002.

Arlen on the streets of Sturgis, South Dakota, 1988.

not making the high-school team. Vacations weren't a regular thing for the family, but they would occasionally get out of town to visit Arlen's uncle Porter in Russian River, which Arlen describes as "a little chicken-shit resort town a hundred miles away." By 1951, when Arlen was in seventh grade, his dad purchased a truck to start his own furniture delivery business, and they moved into the first house they actually owned, which was in San Leandro.

Arlen was an only child until his younger brother, Kevin, was born in 1954. By that time, between school and a good job he had in a furniture store after school and on weekends, Arlen was rarely home. This wasn't his first work experience. Back in junior high school, Arlen would hang out at a San Lorenzo bowling alley and make 10 cents a game by setting pins—this was before the advent of pin-setting machines. He opened a savings account with his earnings, and today, over 50 years later, with commercial bank accounts in the millions of dollars, he's still with the same bank.

Arlen heartily accepted Ervin and Elaine's strong work ethic. He enjoyed working, saw its merits, and has worked continuously ever since that very first job. School never seemed quite so important, although he never considered leaving before graduation. He went to his classes and completed his assignments, but his grades were just mediocre.

Outside school, sports had been the closest thing he had to a hobby until he discovered the fun on East 14th Street between San Leandro and Oakland. It was the 1950s, and the car-club rage of Southern California had moved up the coast. Arlen remembers, "I used to go by the Quarter Pound [burger joint] starting when I was in high school. Guys hung out there. There were always club guys with a line of bobbers out front. We'd park and I'd get a burger and go walk around to check them out, thinking how I would love to have one. I did that right up until I got married." This was where and when Arlen first developed his love of cars and bikes, particularly those that were tweaked and modified. He spent many nights on the strip cruising in friends' cars and later, in his own. They listened to R&B on the radio as they drove around visiting friends at drive-ins like Gordon's and Hap's.

With a job and money coming in and only one year till he could get his driver's license, Arlen now had a goal: buying his own car. He sold the Cushman scooter he owned and loved during eighth grade and added the money to his savings. By the time he was a high-school freshman, he had enough money in the bank to buy a 1947 torpedo-back Oldsmobile, and shortly after, a 1951 Merc that got him and his friends around for the next few years.

The Merc was the car he was driving when as a senior, a neighborhood friend, Mel Pacheco, organized a drive to go see Mt. Diablo after a freak storm covered it in snow. It was an opportunity for Mel to introduce Arlen to a friend of his from the Catholic high school he attended. Bev Rego was two years younger than Arlen and came from a more conservative family, but Arlen was immediately interested. That first outing was followed with many hour-long phone calls and requests to date. Bev repeatedly turned him down until she finally accepted an invitation to go to San Francisco on a Sunday afternoon. It was

Catholic, but as Bev told her mother, "It's not like I'm going to marry the guy."

After graduating from high school, Arlen immediately started working for the post office. As was the practice, he had to substitute for absent mail carriers, almost always walking their routes, until his own route became available. The postal job allowed Arlen to save enough money to buy a 1951 Cadillac convertible, which he promptly lowered and modified with different exhaust pipes. He wanted to do much more to that car, but he was on a limited budget, so he had to take it to Mexico to have it upholstered with tuck and roll, the big deal in those days.

actually a double date to the San Francisco Zoo with Mel and his girlfriend. One date followed another until they were officially boyfriend and girlfriend.

If a school dance or game was going on, Arlen and Bev would go. But for real dates, which Bev's parents would allow only once a week, they would go to the same place over and over again. Bev recalls, "We did the cruising scene up and down East 14th to the drive-ins. We would just cruise on in, and someone would come out and wait on us at the car. We just went for a Coke and fries or a coffee. We'd go from drive-in to drive-in because everyone just loved to look at the cars. Everyone there had cool cars and they were all immaculate. It was a cool thing." Bev's parents weren't too happy about their dating and especially about Arlen not being

After two years of dating and just two months after Bev graduated from high school, the couple was married in August, 1959. Arlen turned 20 the month before and Bev was still 17. Not being 21 yet, their parents had to sign the marriage license for them. Following the afternoon church ceremony, there was a party for 300 for which Bev's family did all the cooking.

Licensed goods and toys have become part of the Ness Lineup, Dublin, California, 2004.

Arlen's brother Kevin with Sherri, Corey, and Bev's brother Steve, 1968.
Ness Family archive

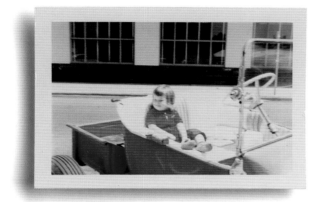

Sherri in Arlen's T-Bucket Roadster, San Lorenzo, California, 1963.
Ness Family archive

When it was all over, Arlen and Bev drove off in Ervin's newer Cadillac for a one-week honeymoon to Carmel and down the coast to L.A., where they took a boat to Catalina Island for a couple of days. They took his dad's car because it was more likely to get them there and back.

Arlen and Bev returned to their jobs and a previously rented apartment after the honeymoon. Their new home was a flat-top duplex on Graham Court in San Leandro that Arlen had already furnished. With just one car, Arlen would drop Bev off at work each day on the way to his government job. She was working as a stenographer in the personnel department at the Chevrolet plant. They both worked hard and saved. Ninety percent of Bev's paycheck went straight into savings bonds. Arlen had already put quite a bit away

before getting married, so their savings grew quickly. Their plan was to buy their own house and start a family.

Life was good for the newlyweds in the 1960s. While this would be the decade that rocked America's institutions, the Ness family concentrated on work and home and didn't get involved in the social changes that would transform our country. They had enough to deal with minding their own business and just growing up. Their entertainment included visiting friends, cruising East 14th Street, and getting a burger on Friday nights. Then in October, 1961, their first child, Sherri, was born. Bev had to leave work when she was six months pregnant, a common workplace practice at the time, but she went back (after shedding many tears) when Sherri was six weeks old. "I hated taking her to the babysitter every day, even though I had a great gal but I always felt it was something I should be doing," she said. By then, Arlen had given up his postal job for a better opportunity: working full-time for his father. He had already been helping his dad deliver furniture while still at the post office so he understood the business.

The hard work was starting to pay off. In 1962, Arlen and Bev purchased a small 1,100-square-foot three-bedroom house on Bengal Street in San Lorenzo that Bev's grandparents owned. Bev recalls, "It was exciting. It had always been our dream to buy our own house. We just saved our money and put everything toward it so our payment would be something we could afford." The young mom was content at home; besides she was only 20 and had another year before she would be old enough to go out with Arlen for a drink! As a young dad, Arlen's one vice was bowling and, of course, what surrounded bowling. He loved the sport and was very good at it. This meant late nights "pot" bowling for money, a stash of cash in his pocket, and often, a few drinks out with the guys.

UNTOUCHABLE

UNTOUCHABLE

***Untouchable* is often described as Arlen's first bike.** This is true to the extent that, in those years, Arlen would rebuild his own bike year after year because it was all he could afford. What started as a slightly modified used Knucklehead—bought for $300 in 1963—was rebuilt and repainted each year until it took the shape of this extreme custom in 1977. Along the way, it appeared with Sportster and Tombstone gas tanks, had high bars and drag bars, was purple, yellow, and blue, and even had a 1960s-style depiction of his wife Bev on

the gas tank for a few years. The 74-inch motor was eventually taken up to 100 cubic inches with S&S flywheels and big bore barrels. It was joined with a Magnuson supercharger, fed by twin Weber carburetors, and put into one of several small-diameter 5/8-inch Jim Davis chrome-moly frames that were made exclusively for Arlen's use. Not caring for the stock transmission, Arlen cut a Sportster motor in half so he could take the mono-construction tranny from it and join it to the Knucklehead bottom end with a rubber drive belt. What

appears to be an oil bag under the seat is really just a battery box. The oil was hidden in a long tank welded to the top bar under the gas tank. A one-off springer front end was narrowed and used smaller diameter tubing to add to the long lean look. Final finish includes pieces of silver that were heavily engraved, gold-plated, and then riveted to the knuckle rockers and the cam cover. A Dick DeBenedictis–theme graphic decorates the top of the tank.

VL CHOPPER

Arlen bought a brand new 74-cubic inch generator shovelhead motor from a local Harley-Davidson shop for this custom in 1969. His plan? Build a VL Chopper just because he "thought it was cool." He had to cut the top bar off the old flathead frame to accommodate the newer shovelhead design. It was this frame that Arlen copied to make the chrome-moly single down tube VL-style frame that he started selling. The springer front end started life as a stock H-D springer that was narrowed and refabricated 4-inches longer as was common at the time. The drag bars and Sportster-style tanks were also popular. Arlen, or possibly his little brother Kevin, laced the 16-inch rear and 21-inch front wheels before sending them to the chromer, which is how they assembled all of the wheels. The VL Chopper is one of a number of Arlen's early bikes that he restored to their original finish in the 1990s.

PETER MAX BIKE

The Peter Max bike started life as a customer bike in 1969. Arlen did the molding, cut the frame, did the raking, and painted the base coat black. This short bar-hopper bike with the Sportster tank raised high on the top bar was one of Arlen's favorite styles. The raised tank inspired him to develop the "rams horn" handlebars, which came up high and back over the gas tank, yet were still in tight to keep the look. The bike was set up with 21-inch front and 16-inch rear spoked wheels, Ness-fabri-

cated springer, oil bag, and struts, and is powered by an early 900-cc Sportster motor. While dated 1969, the year the bike was started, it wasn't actually assembled until twenty years later when Arlen bought the parts back from the original owner.

TWO BAD

TWO BAD

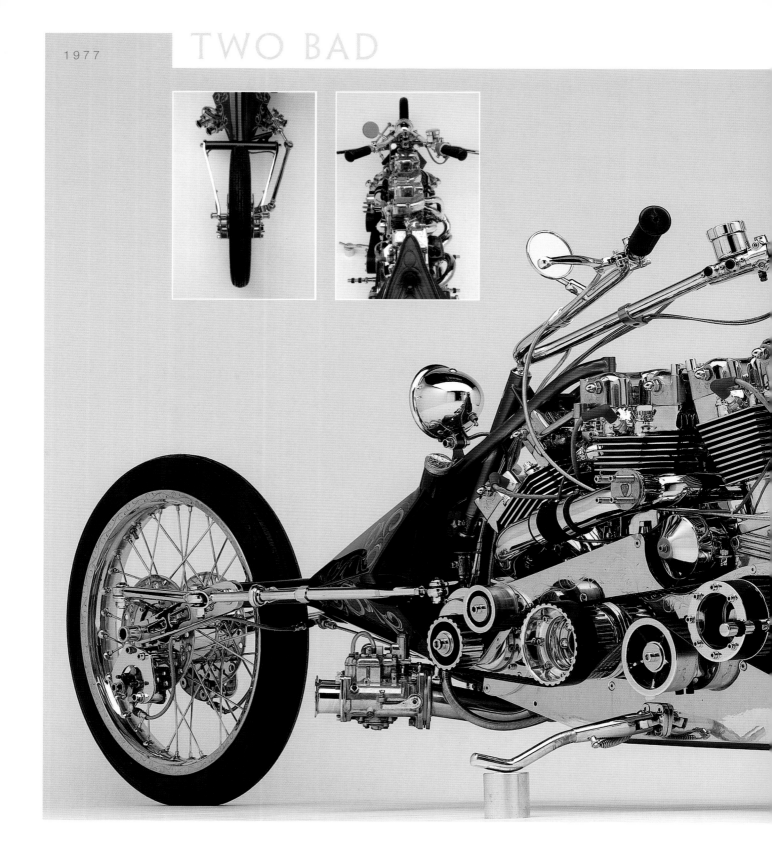

When Arlen built this 2,000-cc twin-engined Sportster in 1987, he went wild with torsion bar suspension, center hub steering, a Magnuson supercharger, two Weber carburetors, two batteries, four gas tanks, incredible paint, gold leaf, twisted exhaust pipes, and details that didn't stop. It debuted at the Oakland Roadster Show in January after friends—including Donnie Smith, Dave Perewitz, Barry Cooney, Arlin Fatland, and Francis Dias—offered last minute help to make the show deadline. Bikers at the

show would jump back as this unattended beast would seemingly start by itself. Arlen's group of friends were having a good laugh in the distance, remote in hand! Two months after the debut, *Two Bad* took first place in the Harley-Davidson ride-in show in Daytona for which Arlen was awarded a handmade Cartier trophy. When Donnie Smith said of Arlen, "He's done everything from the street diggers to the tall choppers to the baggers to two blowers to two motors to two belts to too much!" he was clearly thinking of this bike.

NESS-TIQUE

NESS-TIQUE

After receiving the 1st place trophy (which was a silver model of the original 1903 H-D motorcycle) at the Harley-Davidson ride-in show, Arlen was immediately inspired to build an antique-looking modern custom, something very light and very different. While this has since become a popular motif amongst builders, Arlen had never seen it done before *Ness-tique*. The frame was made by Jim Davis with small-diameter chrome-moly 5/8-inch tubing that was only used for Arlen's personal bikes. To add to the light look, parts were cut, like the fins from the bottom of the barrels and the bottom of the kicker cover, and Danny Gray made as small a seat as was possible. The two 21-inch wheels seem to finish the antique look that everybody loves. *Ness-tique* is one of the bikes that Arlen sold earlier in his career and was lucky enough to buy back for his collection years later.

A $300 KNUCKLEHEAD

WHILE delivering furniture in Oakland one day, Arlen pulled over to get a closer look at an old Harley-Davidson that was for sale outside a cement yard. The bike was behind a fence, so he couldn't look too closely, but he liked what he could see and wrote down the phone number from the sign. It had "fat bob" tanks and a Springer front end, but there was also some chrome so you knew it had been fixed up a bit. That same night, Arlen called the owner, got some more information, and made arrangements to meet. For some unknown reason, this young, quiet, conservative dad just had to have that bike, even if it meant going against the wishes of the people who were closest too him.

Arlen had ridden a Harley before. According to his brother-in-law Richard Rego, Arlen used to occasionally ride a Harley owned by his cousin Kim as early as 1959. But the prejudice against motorcycles was strong at that time. Hardly anyone liked motorcycles, especially big, loud V-twins. Arlen's family intensely disliked them. His dad had forbid him from buying a bike when he was younger because he felt, like most people did, that they were too associated with the outlaw image. These were the years when Hollywood portrayed bikers as outlaws in films like *The Wild One* (1954), *Motorcycle Gang* (1957), and *Dragstrip Riot* (1958). The only reason he allowed Arlen to have a Cushman to ride around the block back when he was younger was because he didn't see it as a motorcycle at all. Then there was Bev, who shared Ervin's sympathies; she may have been even more negative about bikes.

The next day, Arlen went to meet the owner without telling anyone except his friend Charlie, who went with him. The bike was a 1947 Knucklehead that had been stripped down a bit but was all there. They weren't there very long before Arlen offered $300 cash and the deal was closed. As Arlen tells the story, Charlie rode the bike "from Oakland to San Lorenzo to his house. Then I rode it from his house to my house, which wasn't very far. I remember killing that thing a dozen times, at almost every stop sign. It had a suicide clutch, and I didn't know how to ride with one. But I finally got it home, pulled into the driveway, and racked it up. The garage door was open. Bev opened the kitchen door into the garage and she sees me out there on the bike. She knew. She just slammed the door."

By then, there was no turning back. Arlen had made a decision, and he was going to stick with it. He parked the bike and went in to

The original Knucklehead in front of Arlen's house after he first customized it. San Lorenzo, California, c. 1964.
Ness Family archive

a cold shoulder. Days went by before Bev spoke to him again. "She's plenty stubborn," Arlen says about Bev, "but I did what I wanted to do whether she liked it or not; I lived my own life, too. I'm sure there were some arguments." Eventually, Bev acknowledged that there was nothing she could do to change Arlen's mind, and he was already reworking that Knucklehead to make it his own. When the bike was ready to cruise East 14th Street, it had a peanut-style gas tank, apehangers, and a metal-flake green paint job that was Arlen's very first. The bike was a hit, and in no time at all people began asking Arlen to paint their bikes. Within a few months, Arlen's brother-in-law Rich bought a 1947 Knucklehead as well. The two saw each other almost every day, since Arlen delivered furniture for the store where Rich worked, getting Rich caught up in the excitement. The two were now riding buddies, and while they were out having fun their wives started spending more time together, too.

Arlen was enjoying the bike, the bowling, and the nights out, but from Bev's perspective he was enjoying them a little too much. When Sherri was just 17 months old and Bev was four months pregnant with their son, Cory, Bev needed a break. The pregnancy was tough on her, and since she'd have to leave work in another month anyway, she decided to quit right then. Her grandmother,

who had been visiting from Hawaii, where Bev was raised, was flying home, so Bev decided to take Sherri and fly back with her. A two-week visit would be enough time to think things through and to be sure that this was how she wanted to live her life. The trip turned out to be difficult and lasted more than two weeks. Sherri contracted the measles, a highly contagious illness that can be particularly dangerous for pregnant women. And Bev had never had the measles before, which made her susceptible to catching it. Calling Arlen was costly, so they spoke only briefly when they did talk. As things turned out, Bev never caught the measles, Sherri recovered, and they flew back to Oakland after three-and-a-half weeks. By the time they were reunited, they agreed that they missed each other too much and that they would work out any differences. Looking back on those times, both Bev and Arlen say that things weren't perfect, but they worked hard, and things did improve.

While the measles made the Hawaii trip difficult, there was another setback and scare after their return to California. Sherri came down with the mumps, another illness that can be dangerous to pregnant women. This time, Bev did catch the virus, but she was told the risk was only in the first trimester, which she was past. That August, Cory was born, a calm, healthy, happy baby, and this time

Arlen's original Knuckle in his garage on its second rebuild, San Lorenzo, California, c. 1965. *Ness Family archive*

around Bev decided not to go back to work. "Raising my own children was a big priority for me," she says, and she was determined to do just that. Arlen continued to work for his dad and pulled in some extra cash working on other people's bikes in the garage. Another issue that came up after Cory was born was Arlen's third and last review by his local draft board. America's involvement in Vietnam was escalating, but military service wouldn't be in Arlen's future: with a wife and two kids, they never opened his file again.

Arlen rode that '47 Knuck everywhere. He quickly made friends with other riders and got involved in the bike scene. A lot of riders hung out in Harry Brown's Hayward garage. Harry painted bikes and knew his stuff. He had a little business going at home. Ed Wiley would wrench on bikes there during the day, and Harry would paint and assemble them in the evenings, after he went home from his day

job. Arlen improved his own paint, graphics, and flaming techniques by just helping Harry out. He would work on their customers' bikes at Harry's, and then on his own Knuckle, which he could never leave alone, at home. He reworked that bike over and over, although he waited a few years before tearing it totally apart and swapping frames. He bought a second bike, a basket-case Knucklehead, a couple of years later, but this was just something to fix up and make a few bucks on.

All the guys were spending a lot of time together in the garage. As Harry tells it, "Wiley wanted to start a club, so he got permission from all the other clubs in the area first. We couldn't think of a name so that's probably where 'Questionmarks' came from. It was something we started as a bunch of guys who wanted to party together." Arlen joined the club right as it started, just as his brother-in-law Rich did. The patch sewn on the back of

Arlen in his driveway with the original Knucklehead in its second form, San Lorenzo, California, c. 1965. *Ness Family archive*

Arlen's original Knuckle in its second rebuild, painted metal flake magenta, Sacramento Roadster Show, California, 1965.
Ness Family archive

their vests was a big red question mark with a Hayward rocker. They thought people would wonder if they were good guys or bad guys with that question mark on their backs. In the beginning, it was just a riding and building club, similar to the car clubs that were so popular.

As a group, they rode to places like the drag races in Fremont. "Sometimes we'd ride our bikes to Haight Street in San Francisco and over to Berkeley on a Friday night," says Arlen. "It was fun to go watch the hippies with their eyeballs rolling around in the back of their heads and doing all that goofy stuff. I was lucky I never got into any of the drugs. Most everybody else that I ran with did, but I never did any acid or any of that crap. That was good."

Harry confirms that Arlen was that straight: "Arlen didn't get into some of the stuff I would get into. He used to drink, but that was it. I was all over the place in them days, but you couldn't get him to do anything else. He was married and was raising two kids. That was cool about him."

Arlen continued to meet people through riding, the club, and the guys who came by the garage. Tommy T, an Oakland Hells Angel, used to come by and introduced him to other members like Sonny Barger, the chapter president. It was also in the garage that Arlen met Tobie Gene Levingston, the president of

the all-black East Bay Dragons M/C when Harry was flaming the Dragon's helmets. Arlen helped on the project and hit it off real well with Tobie Gene. He was invited to a number of Dragons functions, including a ride to the drags, a club picnic, and the popular club dances. Even though he was probably the only white guy at those dances, he remembers always feeling comfortable there.

This was a period in Arlen's life when he came home late after a few too many drinks on a few too many occasions. Harry remembers, "We'd get together and have a drink or go for a ride. We'd ride to Santa Cruz a lot and hang out on the beach with the surf people. Sometimes we'd hang out at the Quarter Pound or a place called the Washington Club in San Leandro. Around 1968, we also used to go to the Green Lantern Bar that was kind of a meeting place for everyone. We knew the bartender, Don, and his wife, Kelly, who was a go-go dancer. They were real nice people. We'd just hang out, have fun, and party with them. We drank a lot of tequila in those days. I remember one

Arlen's brother-in-law Richard Rego.
Ness Family archive

Harry Brown, a close friend and riding partner who gave Arlen many paint tips on his Knucklehead, Hayward, California, c. 1965.
Ness Family archive

time it was pretty wild and we were pretty drunk. Arlen left the bar and hung a U-turn, and I said, 'Where the hell did Arlen go?' So I look across the street and there he is stuck with his front end in a hedge. He jumped the curb and went right into it. There was mud and dirt flying everywhere from the back tire. He killed it trying to get it out and just laughed. Then he got it going and went on home."

Looking back, Arlen says, "I was young and dumb, thinking I was cool but doing really dumb shit." His behavior came to a head when he went out in the car one night to return at 3:00 a.m. to swap the car for the bike. Bev met him at the door with a bucket of cold water. No problem: he went to the bedroom to change into dry clothes, then to the garage for the bike, but Bev had already thwarted his plans with a pair of hedge clippers. There wasn't a cable on the bike that wasn't all messed up. Arlen's reaction was simple: he had a good laugh and went to bed. At least he was a happy drunk!

By 1966, the Questionmarks were becoming more serious as a riding club. Perhaps because of the time some of the members were spending with the Hells Angels, their own club started to feel like an outlaw club. The Hells Angels were recruiting, so a group decision was made to hang up the Questionmark patch. Those who chose to

Arlen and Bev at the Oakland Roadster Show in the mid-1960s.
Ness Family archive

remain with the club donned the Angel patch with a Hayward Rocker. At that point, Arlen, Rich, Harry, and a number of others left the club scene forever. For Arlen, it could have gone the other way. He was feeling like a biker, but Bev was so conservative that she kept Arlen pretty much on the straight and narrow. He says, "I had some common sense, but I mostly attribute that to Bev. I had a good thing with her, and I didn't want to ruin it." His own vest hung from a hook in the garage for many years.

FENDERED PANHEAD

Stock Indian Motorcycles inspired Arlen to build the
Fendered Panhead. The motif saw some popularity in the years
that followed but there wasn't anything out there like this in 1983.
The motor is a stock H-D Panhead that was rebuilt in-house
and put into a 7/8-inch chrome-moly Jim Davis rigid frame. The
front end is a Ness 2-inch-over-stock springer, it has 19-inch front
and 16-inch rear spoke wheels (laced and trued in-house),
steel fenders hand made by Bob Munroe, and a paintjob by Arlen
with finish graphics by Jeff McCann. While the full fenders
aren't body covers, perhaps this bike was also a prelude to the
bigger body bikes that became the rage in the early 1990s.

HULKSTER

Before building this bike, Arlen made a deal with Hulk Hogan, whom he had been introduced to by his close friend, Tony Carlini: a custom bike would be built for the Hulk to his proportions, used for promotion, and displayed at different venues for a couple of years, after which the bike would be returned to Arlen. The 93-inch Shovelhead-powered bike had a car turbo mounted under the seat and used big Brembo breaks with double calipers on the back to stop the machine, the biggest bike Arlen had made at that time. (He has since built a much larger proportioned bike for Shaq.) Bob Munroe hand fabricated the large seven-gallon aluminum gas tanks and Jim Davis made the 7/8 chrome-moly frame and swingarm. Tony, a talented and recognized painter himself, did the Hulk graphic on top of the tank. The *Hulkster* became Arlen's first celebrity bike, made the covers of many magazines, and went all around the world on tour.

STRICTLY BUSINESS

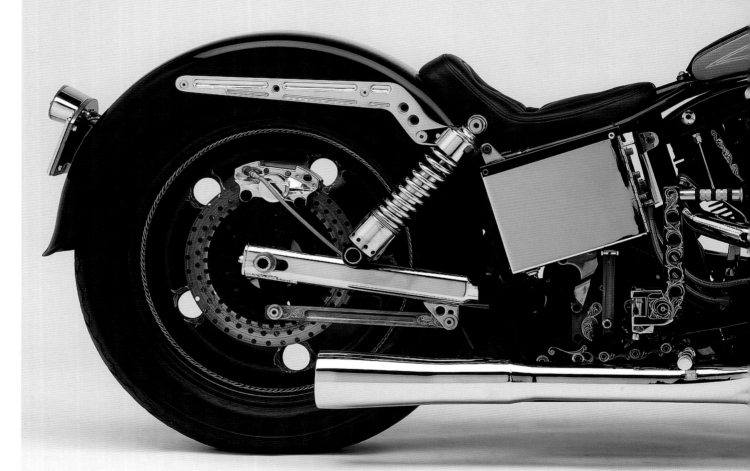

***Strictly Business* started life as Hayward Harley's drag bike.** It was a powerhouse that could run 10.30-second quarter miles. Arlen decided to keep the theme by doing a ground-up rebuild using a Jim Davis/Ness chrome-moly frame, aluminum gas tanks hand fabricated by Bob Munroe, Mitchell race wheels, and two Mikuni smooth-bore carbs to create a really fast street bike. He drilled as much material out of parts as he could to lighten the bike both in weight and looks. The motor had so much compression that Arlen had to stuff very special and very expensive helicopter batteries under the seat to provide the cranking amps needed to start the motor.

The special oval Ness swingarm, handlebars, and triple trees were available through the Ness catalog at the time but most of the bike was one-off and was finished with a lot of hand engraving, a paintjob by Arlen, and Jeff McCann graphics. The bike wasn't only fast; it was fun too. Arlen rode it from his shop to the Redwood Run and from Denver to Sturgis one year.

ORANGE BLOSSOM

Orange Blossom used almost the same frame as Strictly Business, except it was built to accommodate an early Harley-Davidson five-speed transmission and a 93-inch Shovel-Knuckle motor (Shovelhead bottom end with a Knucklehead top end) with special aluminum cylinders. Arlen made as many parts as possible out of aluminum. He drilled them and then sand blasted them, which gave the bike a light and racy look. To hold the fuel, a foundry cast beautiful aluminum gas tanks from an old Henderson tank that Arlen had. The wheels were aluminum alloy with chrome spokes. Arlen rode Orange Blossom from Denver to Sturgis in the summer of 1984. That fall, he rode it into the opening reception of "California Dream" at the Oakland Museum of California, which had two of his bikes on display.

ACCEL BIKE

The 90-ci "Knuckster" motor (Knucklehead top end with Sportster cases) in the street-style digger _Accel Bike_ is a rare powerplant. As far as Arlen knows, it is the only one in existence and was made for him by Ron Trock of Trock Cycle. The fuel tank is incorporated into the top bar of the frame and the oil bag is in the back down tube. Both are made from steel cylinders that were put into a press to achieve the shapes Arlen envisioned. As he did with the contemporary _Orange Blossom_, holes were drilled where possible—including in the 19-inch solid front and rear wheels—to lighten the look. A Honda front end and two sets of smooth-bore carbs (four total) give further credit to this bike's racing roots.

Arlen riding his
Gibson Bike, Livermore
Hills, California, 2004.

THE
BUSINESS TAKES OFF

Kevin helping his
friend Kirk in the 14th
Street store,
San Leandro, California,
c. 1972.
Ness Family archive

IT WAS 1967 and the Summer of Love. Young people from all over the country flocked to San Francisco, just across the bay from where Arlen lived and worked. As with so much else that occurred in the 1960s, Arlen didn't get involved, and while he would still ride over for a look, he mostly minded his own business, which by then was starting to take off. He earned enough side money from the work he was doing in the garage to enable him to buy more tools and motorcycle parts. It was hard to keep up when he had to go to his day job delivering furniture six days a week, and then work long hours on bikes every night. Arlen's little brother was only 12 years old, but Arlen thought he was old enough to help out. He would sometimes pick Kevin up after school and bring him back to the garage, where he could do all sorts of odd jobs. As Kevin tells it, "When I was still in sixth grade in grammar school, I used to work with Arlen in his garage, long before he had his shop. I helped him mold and prime motorcycle frames, or when he went off to his other job, he'd leave me a toolbox and would have me tear apart a highway patrol bike that he had bought. I'd also take apart the wheels and polish the spokes at a workbench where he set up a polisher with a washing-machine

motor. I'd get the spokes ready to go to the plater. Later he showed me how to do base coats. We did everything there in that garage."

There was another young helper who appeared on the scene around the same time. Johnny Lopez was in junior high school when he saw Arlen pull up to his neighbor's house on one of his customs, but he knew right then he wanted to learn more about bikes. Johnny's neighbor was Stanley Ornelis, one of the best stripers in the area, who happened to do a lot of Arlen's work. On one of Arlen's visits, Johnny asked Arlen if he could help out.

"I started going over to Arlen's garage in San Lorenzo. I had to ride my bike or take a bus. I'd go over twice in a week or sometimes just every other week. Occasionally, he would come and get me. At first he had me molding and sanding tanks, which I didn't like too much. I'd go and spend a half a day or more working on stuff. There were a lot of people hanging in his garage then, people I didn't even know. They'd come by to say hi and see what he was doing and what he was up to. Arlen's name would get out for his painting, and guys would bring their bikes over. Ron Simms used to come over there before he had a shop, but I didn't even know who he was till years later. The garage was always open, and

Arlen behind the counter at the first store on 14th Street shortly after opening, San Leandro, California, c. 1971. *Ness Family archive*

Arlen was always doing something. It was a two-car garage with a little paint area out back. I used to tell Arlen this was going to turn into something big, but he just did it because he loved it, the art of the painting and what he could do with his hands. He has never been big-headed about anything either. Everyone was always welcome at his house or the shop."

Most of his time then was devoted to customer's bikes. Arlen recalls how he charged $125 for a paint job, "and that included everything. I'd sandblast the frame, grind away the tabs, and mold the tank with Bondo. When it got fancier with graphics and pinstriping, the price went up because I had to pay someone else to do that. Today,

the $125 wouldn't even come close to paying for the raw paint."

Kevin and Johnny were a big help, but they weren't there all that much, so Arlen still had to do almost everything himself. The work seemed to keep increasing, but there was only so much time to get it done. Arlen thought he found the solution in 1968 when he joined the carpenters union so he could take a new job installing sliding-glass doors and windows. With half-days off on Fridays (a union perk), weekends, and quite a few weather days, there would be much more time to devote to building bikes and his steadily growing side business. This also worked out because his dad, who was not in very good health then, had a couple of other

First store on 14th Street in San Leandro, California, c. 1972. *Ness Family archive*

people working for him. There was enough time now to display a bike at a show here and there, and always at the Oakland Roadster Show, which Arlen felt was the show of shows. Sometimes a photo of one of his bikes at the show would appear in a motorcycle magazine, and he learned from the response that even a small mention in a magazine was a good thing.

Arlen made parts for himself like anyone else who worked on their own bikes. Pre-fabricated aftermarket parts were just becoming available, but for the most part, the guys who knew how kept making their own. Arlen came up with a set of bars for a bike he was building with a Sportster tank mounted way up on the top bar. He had the bars, which he called ram's-horn bars, come up over the tank instead of around it. "People seemed to like them," Arlen says, "so I went down to Superior Tube, and they bent more up for me. Then I'd take these to a polishing shop to have them polished, bring them back to weld the bungs in them, and then I'd take them to the chrome shop. My first production may have been twenty sets. That was a big investment at that time for me to make twenty sets, but people would see my handlebars in a magazine on a bike and they would call up to order them. I didn't know anything about advertising."

It was positive feedback in the form of customers, phone orders, and cash. That first part was followed by a second—drag bars, which Arlen has sold thousands of over the years and continues to sell today. "Every time I would sell a part, I would take the money and buy two parts, since I was living off of my painting." Pretty soon, Arlen thought, "This could be a business." He looked for more products to make. He also started to think that he could make a living by just doing bikes, again if he could just have more time to devote to it.

Something had to give, and this time it was easy. After only a year in the carpenters union, Arlen quit his day job to make motorcycles his full-time business in 1969. Paint was the mainstay, but there was a lot of fab work and parts, too. To be more efficient, he built a room on the back of the house to serve as a paint booth. Up until then, he had to clean the garage by hosing it down before painting. Now it was a real business. Everything seemed to be working as he had hoped, possibly too well. Customers would come by at all hours of the day and night, and it was common to work until midnight. It was a good thing he was at the house so he could see the family. Arlen would go in the house to

Sheri Ness opening a Christmas present. *Ness Family archive*

get various things, Bev, Cory, and Sherri would come out and visit, and Arlen would join them for dinner.

In 1969, as the decade came to a close, Neil Armstrong walked on the moon in July, three days of peace and music happened at Woodstock in August, and back in San Leandro, California, Arlen continued to mind his business as it took off. He did get out every now and again, including one particularly memorable outing in December when he rode his Knuckle to Altamont. As he tells it, "I rode my bike out there to see the Stones with some friends. I remember splitting lanes through traffic for miles and miles and miles with cars just stopped dead everywhere. We were far up on a hill, not by the stage where all the stuff was going on. I didn't know about it until later. It was a wild thing." Of course, he's referring to the famous concert that tried to recapture the earlier magic of Woodstock. What was to turn into a fiasco (resulting in four deaths) was captured by the Maysles brothers in their 1970 documentary film *Gimme Shelter*. Once again, Arlen sailed through amazing times and just kept doing his thing.

Arlen remembers that after starting full-time work in the garage, customers and friends kept coming by the house, keeping him from finishing his work. "They'd come over and bring a jug of wine or a six-pack. I couldn't get any work done, and I needed to work. I had a house payment and two kids." By the end of the year, it was clear that another change was called for. Arlen found the

solution in a small storefront where he could meet customers in the evening. The work would still have to be done in the garage, but at 6:00 p.m. he would go to the storefront. How appropriate that they ended up leasing a space on East 14th Street, right back in the heart of the car and motorcycle culture where he and Bev had spent so much time. "The rent was $75 a month, and I remember when I signed that lease that we were scared to death we wouldn't be able to make the payment. We were open six to ten o'clock or sometimes six to eleven after painting all day at home."

Arlen needed a name for the new, more official looking business, and Bev felt that no matter what they came up with, it should have Arlen's name right in it. Arlen agreed: "Using my own name for the business was the best thing I ever did, because you remember the name.

One of many trophies in the Ness Museum, Dublin, California, 2004.

chopped it, and painted it. He entered it in bike shows, and once he had his license, he'd ride it from school to go open the shop in the afternoon. He sold parts, answered the phone, and did a little ordering until Arlen would arrive with a new paint job for a customer, parts to bring back to the garage, or to take over for the evening.

Just because Arlen had a storefront didn't mean he always had to do business. Arlen loved to ride to bike events like the Frog Jumps up in Angel Camp in the Sierra foothills or to weekend runs at the Highlands Bar in Clear Lake. He would leave the shop with a pack of bikes and join up with more as they went.

It was on one of these runs in 1970 that Arlen met the painter Horst for the first time. Horst claims he was hardly a painter at the time. "I was riding my first bike," Horst says, "a 650 Kawasaki, which was an exact copy of a pre-unit BSA. I welded a hardtail on it and painted it with a spray can, and then painted it over and over. That's the bike I was riding when we rode up to Clear Lake. I remember Arlen riding alongside. He looked at me and just shook his head." It must have been quite a sight the way Horst describes it. Shortly after this, he bought his first Harley, a bike with a Harry Brown paint job that lasted only a week before Horst repainted it. He went on to do a number of paint jobs for Arlen and has come to be recognized as one of the great painters in the business.

We called it 'Arlen's Motorcycle Accessories,' only 'Arlen's' was really the name of the shop. My name on the sign was three times bigger than 'Motorcycle Accessories.' Almost everybody else had custom shops that didn't use their own names."

That December, Arlen, Bev, and Kevin hung the sign over the door at 15540 East 14th Street. In January, 1970, they opened for business. In the years that followed, they played on Arlen's name with sayings like "Arlen's Motorcycle Ness-essities," and "Ness" got incorporated into the names of many bikes like *Smooth-Ness*, *Team Ness* and *Ness-Stalgia*. Arlen was right; everyone remembers his name.

Kevin turned 16 just before the shop opened, which meant he was old enough to have a license. Arlen had bought him a 350-cc Honda basket case when he turned 15, so in his spare time, Kevin raked the neck,

BLOWER BIKE

BLOWER BIKE

Blower Bike **was Arlen's first bike to have aluminum bodywork, in the form of louvered side panels, rear fender panels, and fairing insets.** He used flattened large-diameter steel tubing, as he had done the year before on *Accel Bike*, to replace the top bar as a fuel tank. As with *Accel Bike*, this bike has a Honda front end and 19-inch front and rear wheels, although these wheels are spoked and have a louvered hubcap over the back wheel. At almost 8 inches, the rear road-racing tire was a very wide tire for the day. To make a wheel that could support it, Arlen had to weld two halves of a 19-inch front rim onto a 16-inch rear wheel. A rubber belt transferred power from the 93-inch Shovelhead motor to the tranny, and dual-caliper Brembo brakes on the rear could bring the bike to a quick stop. While almost every piece of the bike was hand fabricated, there were several parts like the fairing (at least an unenhanced version of it), handlebars, front fender, and triple clamps that were available through the Ness catalog.

METZELER BLUE SHOVEL

With the exception of just a few years around 1990, Arlen has had a nearly exclusive relationship with Avon Tires. This particular bike, which was built during that two-year period, featured Metzeler tires and was used by the tire company in an ad and poster campaign. It employed an 80-inch Shovelhead motor with a five-speed tranny that he had lying around the shop. Asked recently whether he would consider putting a Shovel in a new bike, Arlen replied,

"No. They were shit motors." And that's not because it's an older motor; he wouldn't hesitate to use an even older Pan or Knuckle. The bike was built on a stock FXR frame before he came out with his own Ness version. Arlen customized it with a front stretch by sectioning the tubing in front of the top motor mount down to the foot controls. Stock fat bob gas tanks were narrowed to give the bike a racier look that went with the Ness sport bike–style fairing and aluminum side panels. The tires were mounted to 19-inch front and 16-inch rear wheels, and, to carry the tire sponsor's theme to the surface, the tread pattern was painted on top of the fenders.

NESS CAFÉ

This cute little bar hopper appropriately made the cover of *Cycle World* in June 1991. It started life as a stock Harley-Davidson XR 1000, a bike Arlen never really liked the looks of. His approach was to take the bike, which he bought as a wreck from Canada, and redress it by stretching the swingarm, raking the neck, combining two stock gas tanks to make fat bob sporty tanks, putting a

Ness fairing out front, and adding aluminum side panels and a front scoop. For better performance, the stock brakes were replaced with Performance Machine brakes, and a set of Mikuni carbs replaced the originals. The tread pattern appears on the fender as it did a year earlier on the *Metzeler Blue Shovel*. Arlen chose to ride *Ness Café* for a full season because it was such a good-handling light bike.

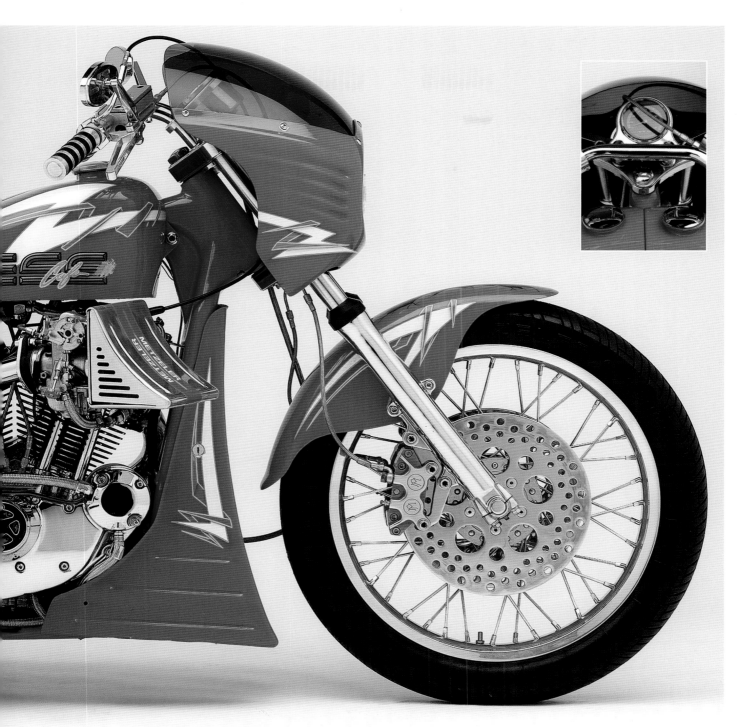

FERRARI BIKE

Work on *Ferrari Bike* started in 1987 after Arlen had some of his ideas transferred to paper in the form of drawings, something he had never done before. He had already visited the Ferrari factory in Italy and had customized a Ferrari 308 to look similar to a Testerosa, only "cooler and better" than the original. *Ferrari Bike* fit well with his car. To help bring his vision to life, Craig Naff, who was working for Boyd Coddington, was employed to shape all of the bodywork, which he did so well that Arlen rode the bike for quite some time in bare aluminum. The bike was ahead of its time in many ways. It preceded the body bikes that appeared several years later. It pioneered the use of wide motorcycle tires that came into vogue almost ten years later. Because nothing appropriate was commercially available for the back wheel, Arlen mounted a car tire on a modified car rim. The bike is powered by a rare 122-inch Harmon motor. It is also equipped with twin Magnuson blowers, one for each head, two nitrous bottles, four Weber carbs, special perimeter brakes, and two rear belts that transfer power to the back wheel. While Arlen rode the bike 300 miles to the Redwood Run in one day and at many other motorcycle events, he won't try to tell you it is an easy ride. A day on it wore him out, but it was worth it for the attention it received.

YELLOW KNUCKLEHEAD CHOPPER

This sweet little rigid custom that Arlen built "just for fun" used a stock 74-inch Harley-Davidson Knucklehead motor and ratchet-top transmission that he had lying around. It was one of three yellow bikes Arlen built at the same time, a chopper, a bagger, and a hot rod FXR. Arlen used a foot shift instead of the original jockey shift that would have been used with the Knucklehead motor. The 21-inch front wheel fits well in the Ness-Allington–made springer front end and was complemented by a skinny 18-inch rear wrapped in a lengthened tail-dragging fender. The high bars were mounted low to give them a taller look while possibly avoiding a high-bar ticket. Without the usual Ness rake on the front end, this chopper sports a short, responsive bar-hopping look.

San Leandro Park.

THE NEXT STEP

THERE was a big change in how Arlen looked at the business during that first year on East 14th Street. A number of things happened that had an impact on him, including an encounter with "a guy in the army who got a re-enlistment bonus check for $2,200. He came in and bought a bunch of parts from me. I made $100 profit on that stuff in one day when my rent was still $75 a month. It was the biggest sale I'd ever made. If I could do this all the time, I'd be shitting in tall cotton and a millionaire in no time. Bev and I went to Banchero's Restaurant to celebrate and still had money left over."

Arlen was starting to think bigger. It wasn't just the shop; it probably had more to do with meeting Larry Kumferman, the editor of *Custom Bike Magazine*. Larry loved what Arlen was doing and really helped him out. He started putting Arlen and his bikes in the magazine, and Arlen's world grew very quickly. When the phone rang, it could as easily be someone on the East Coast or in the Midwest as someone down the road in Hayward. This was the beginning of a long ride with the media.

Arlen liked selling parts, and his strategy of "bigger, better, and more" was working. It was time for Arlen to head out to Walnut Creek so he could "meet Jim Davis to see

about him making custom frames for me. Someone told me he was the guy that could make anything. He could even make a machine to make anything. He built the first rear-engine dragsters, but then the dragster business got slow, and he had such an incredible reputation for his welding. I wanted a stretched rigid Sportster frame for myself and to sell. There was hardly anyone making any frames at that time, so I took a stock Sportster frame out there with a swingarm and shocks on it, lay it over on the cement floor, took a yardstick and chalk and stretched it so far here, so far there. Then Davis built a chrome-moly frame like it. The state-of-the-art chrome-moly steel flexes, is stronger, and no one had made frames from it before this. Everybody else was making them out of seamed tubing. I had them made in 7/8-inch but made it in 5/8-inch for my own bikes." From then on, Arlen would order at least 10 or 20 frames at a time from Jim. His stable of California craftsmen was growing.

That first meeting with Jim led to years of collaboration and a very close personal friendship. And there was someone else at that meeting: Bob Munroe. Bob, who has always been known as "Mun," was working for Jim in the shop and also became a close friend of Arlen's. Mun started his own shop a few years

Arlen and Jim Davis in Jim's shop, Brentwood, California, 1987.

later and took over the sheet-metal fabrication of gas tanks, oil bags, and fenders, leaving the frames for Jim. Neither Jim nor Mun rode when they first met Arlen, but with their backgrounds, they took to riding quickly.

Arlen also sold springer-style front ends. He had been buying up old stock Springers and fixing them up, but they were getting harder and harder to find. Arlen had heard that a guy named Steve Allington, who owned a shop called Cycleology in Fremont, could help him, so he went out to pay Steve a visit.

As Steve recalls, "Arlen came down to the shop in a lowered black Cadillac that I thought was very cool. He came in and said 'I'm Arlen Ness,' and he started buying parts from me, mainly front ends and mainly Springers. He would sell them under his name. It got to the point that he would buy one hundred front ends raw from me, and then he would chrome them and assemble them."

As with most of the people Arlen worked with, they rode together, hung out, and became friends. Steve went on about those early days: "We would go out and get blitzed in bars and open up bowling alleys at four

in the morning to bowl and come home at seven when it's light out. We would do dumb things and have fun. It is just the way it was." And somehow, they both were able to take care of business.

The store was working out great for Arlen, and the timing couldn't have been more perfect. Business grew steadily just as custom biking grew in popularity, and a new industry was developing to support the interest. The stage had been set in the 1960s when a cluster of biker movies was released, but it wasn't until Peter Fonda and Dennis Hopper went looking for America in the film *Easy Rider* (1969) that the fuse was lit. Today it would be hard to find a rider over 50 who didn't see it right when it was released. Arlen says, "*Easy Rider* was a big influence on motorcycles. I remember going to the drive-in and seeing the movie. We all went on the bikes one night. I thought the movie was pretty cool. I thought all that stuff was pretty cool.

Bob "Mun" Munroe.

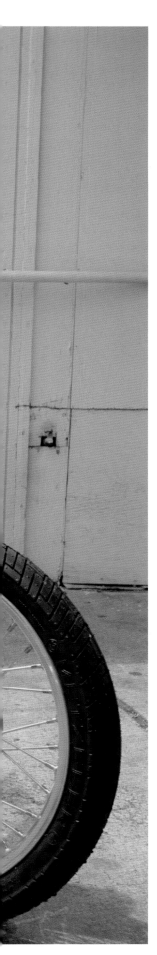

Red Flame Chopper is one of a series of choppers that Arlen built from parts he had lying around his shop. They were built for fun and for himself, mostly after dinner right into the night. Inspired by his original Knucklehead, the choppers were simple, easy-to-ride high-bar bikes that recall the 1960s with an updated flare. Arlen chose an 80-ci Shovelhead motor with an S&S carb to power this bike. Since he discontinued Ness springers by the early 1990s, he used a short Paucho springer with a 21-inch front wheel. The high bars were mounted low on the front end, similar to the *Yellow Knucklehead Chopper* from 1990. There was extra sheet metal for Arlen to work his flame magic on as he cupped the Sportster tanks over the motor and back around the seat, lengthened the oil bag right to the rear axle, and made a one-off fiberglass tail-dragger fender that nearly touched the ground and wrapped right in toward the tire. The flames were actually three separate sets that give a wild, busy look to the bike. Long modified Ness running boards make the bike particularly comfortable to ride, which may be why Arlen still takes it out quite a bit. He recently rode it around L.A. while he was filming an episode of the television show *Big*.

MONO LISA

There is a classic beauty about this long, sleek bike that makes its name doubly appropriate. Its open rear fender looks back on a following rider like the eyes of the similarly named painting, but it isn't really the painting the name refers to. While it has appeared in print as *Mona Lisa*, the correct name of *Mono Lisa* refers to Arlen's unusual suspension, which features a mono shock placed vertically under the seat to experiment with a Softail-looking rubber-mount frame design. The bike was made from a stock 80-inch Evo motor, a five-speed FXR tranny, and 19-inch front and 18-inch rear chrome aluminum wheels fitted with PM rotors and European six-piston calipers. What really stands out is how the all-aluminum body works with the elongated tank, air cleaner, running boards, fenders, and trim to add more length to the bike. As the last Metzeler-affiliated bike, the open back fender was more than just a design consideration.

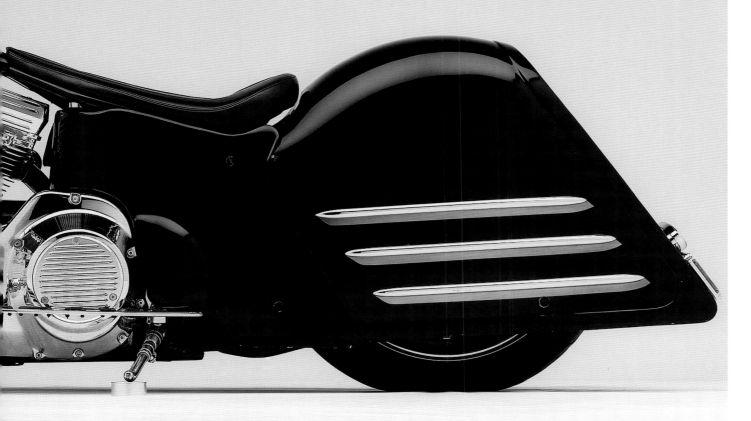

NESS-STALGIA

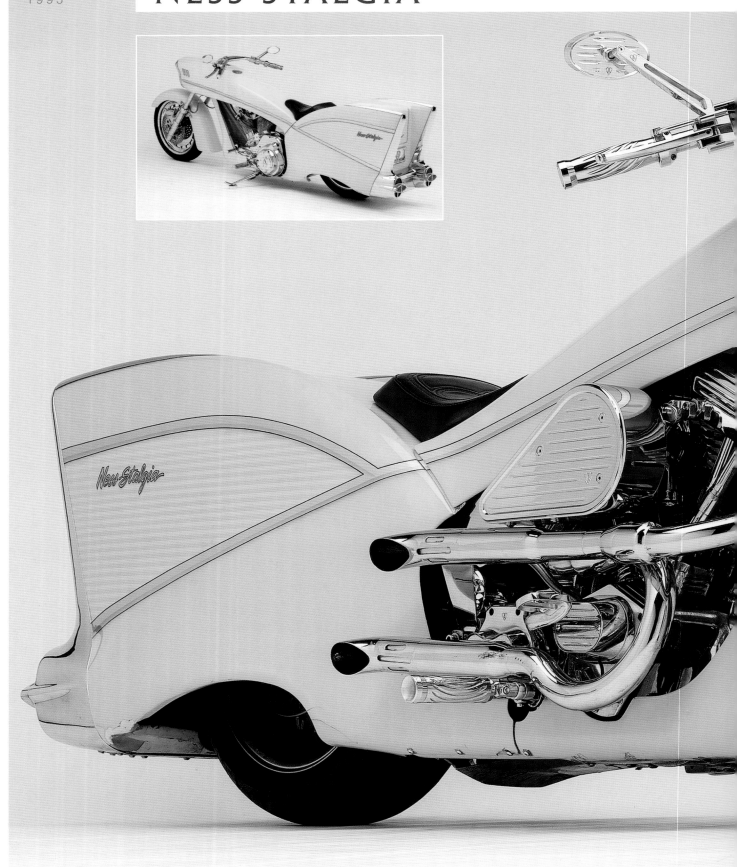

NESS-STALGIA

Ness-Stalgia is often referred to as the Chevy Bike with its styling reminiscent of a 1957 Chevrolet. It was Arlen's first major theme bike and is the result of a group of drawings Carl Brouhard brought to Arlen in 1993. The frame was another experiment for Arlen, with shocks hidden underneath the bike. It has a 38-degree rake, five-inch front stretch and two-inch rear stretch, and is one of about ten similar frames Arlen made for his own use. The motor is a stock Evo. Bob Munroe made the

pipes, Danny Gray the seat, and the 18-inch rear and 19-inch front wheels are from Performance Machine. Ron Covel hand formed the amazing aluminum body including the bumpers, fins, and trim. Carl was brought back in to do the trompe l'oeil paint job. It is difficult to tell whether you are looking at paint or chrome on certain parts of the bodywork, and the trunk looks like it can really open. While this bike started as a fun project for Arlen, it was so well received that it is considered one of his signature bikes. Those who can remember a real '57 Chevy especially appreciate this bike.

SMOOTH-NESS

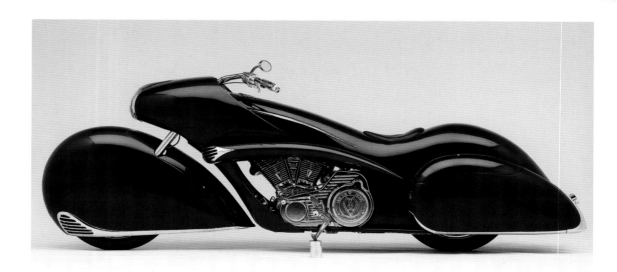

The art deco design of *Smooth-Ness* makes this bike one of Arlen's favorites. It is based on a sculpture of a 1932 Bugati Roadster that Arlen has in his house. The lines of the sculpture and of an actual Bugati were well translated into Carl Brouhard's initial 1993 sketches, and Craig Naff's hand-formed aluminum body and trim. Craig's workmanship was so perfect that Arlen rode this bike unpainted at several rallies. At the heart of the flowing forms that wrap around another experimental Ness rubber-mount Softail frame is a stock 80-inch H-D Evo motor tied to a stock FXR tranny. It provides all the power Arlen feels the bike needs. Even though so little can be seen of them, 21-inch front and 18-inch rear wheels were selected. The minimalist seat was by Danny Gray, as are almost all of Arlen's seats. Not only was Carl instrumental with his sketches and designs at the outset of *Smooth-Ness*, he was also provided the final paint, just in time to meet the January 1995 deadline for the Oakland Roadster Show. The matching helmet also debuted at the same time.

BUILDERS GATHER, THE HAMSTERS M/C

LOOKING back on Arlen's work of the 1970s, we now see that he had an incredible business model, but at the time he never saw it that way. It would be another 30 years before he would even think about making a business plan. His life and business moved forward one day at a time, one project at a time. With each bike and each magazine article, his recognition grew. After Arlen started appearing in national magazines, he began to travel to bike shows and events outside of California. The first time he was paid to travel somewhere was to Detroit in April, 1974, to a show in Cobo Hall, simply called "Detroit." Arlen was the celebrity judge, and the legendary DJ Wolfman Jack was there to present the trophies. It was at this show where Arlen first met Dave Perewitz, who had a bike on display. By the end of the show, Dave had been called up by Wolfman to receive the Best Paint trophy, and Dave had invited Arlen go back east to the Laconia, New Hampshire, rally in June.

Bob Dron was a friend (and competitor) of Arlen's who was also invited to the Detroit show. Bob opened his American Chopper Enterprises bike shop in Concord, California, the same month Arlen opened his shop and was known as more of a "chopper guy." Bob recalls getting his invitation to Detroit:

"I refused unless they sent me the money first. Arlen said he was going, and I told him he was crazy. Bike shows are usually dollar flops, and who knows if you would get the money they promised, but he went back there. When he got back, he said, 'You won't believe it. They were coming up to me, and one guy kissed my shoes. After the show, they paid me.'" Now, as owner of one of the most successful dealerships in the world, Oakland Harley-Davidson, Bob acknowledges that you had to take those risks back then to make it, but that wasn't Bob's way.

That June, Arlen took Dave Perewitz up on his earlier invitation and made his first trip to the East Coast. He flew into Boston, where Dave and his wife, Susan, picked him up at the airport. Dave recalls: "On the trip to Laconia, we were in my old van, me, Arlen, and Susan. Susan was driving. Of course we had to stop and get a bottle of tequila, and by the time we got up there, boy, were we hammered. I never drank tequila before. About twenty miles before we got to the Weirs, I had to pee, so we pulled over, and I just fell out of the van. I got back in and passed out before we made it to the cabin. When I finally woke up, I was in the cabin, the bikes were unloaded, and my back pocket was ripped off and my wallet was gone. I had a lot of money in it, so the three of us got back into the van and drove to the very spot I fell out of the truck and sure enough, even though it was heavy woods, I found the wallet."

When the rally was over, Arlen suggested to Dave that they go to Detroit instead of back to Brockton. So off they went, their two bikes loaded up in the back of Dave's van, to visit Tony Carlini, the well-known bike painter who they both became friendly with on their trip to the Detroit show that past winter. Arlen planned to leave his digger-style bike, *Silver Lady,* in Detroit with Tony to be photographed for a magazine and then picked up by a customer. He still regrets having sold *Silver Lady,* but those were the days you just could-n't afford to keep bikes. Unfortunately, his attempts at buying the bike back have never been successful.

Silver Lady happened to be the last bike that Kevin worked on with Arlen. Kevin explains: "I left because I was getting into partying and having some marriage problems. I got hooked up with the wrong people and got into drugs, drinking, women, and running around. It just wasn't working. I was coming in late, I was doing motors at home, and that wasn't working either. It was a big party. I left the shop and didn't do anything for about a year. I'd just sell a car or a bike when I needed some cash. Eventually, I became a diesel mechanic and made some good money and eventually got a job at a cemetery where I hand-made bronze urns."

Looking back, Kevin now says, "Arlen was always against drugs. Ever since I was in grammar school, he beat that into me. I've learned over the years growing up that if he said, 'Don't do it,' and I did it, he was always right, but you have to learn the hard way. Now, I listen to him pretty close and take his advice." In 1975, Kevin and Arlen decided that his lifestyle didn't mix with the shop, nor

with how Arlen ran things, and they mutually decided that Kevin should move on.

Business continued to grow every year for Arlen. He was always branching out and trying new things. He had been doing a catalog for several years, but as Arlen says, "It was really just a flier. Bev knew how to type, so she typed it up. It had the name of each product and the price, like the ram's-horn handlebars and how much they were. We didn't even have part numbers then. There may have been half a dozen products, that's it. Then Jeff McCann got involved and

Ness-tique sits in front of Bob Dron's first Harley store in Oakland, California, 1987.

helped do the next one, since he knew how to do that."

Jeff had been helping Arlen since they met back in 1970. He opened his bike shop the very same month as Arlen opened his, and apparently Arlen had gone over to sell him some parts. Jeff ordered two of everything he had, and then Arlen started buying parts from him. After opening several stores, Jeff ran into some problems and closed his business in 1975. Because he had a background in printing and graphics, it seemed natural that Arlen, as Jeff tells, "asked me to help him do a catalog in late 1976. So I took all the pictures, wrote the copy, produced it, and had it printed by a local company. It was saddle-stitched with a two-color cover and black-and-white printing on the inside. They were produced as inexpensively as we could at the time." Many more products were added to this bigger catalog, including some Jim Davis frames and some of Mun's diamond and rocket gas tanks.

Arlen working on a metal lathe in his shop at the Castro Valley house, 1987.

The look of Arlen's bikes from that time can be summed up in *Untouchable*, the 1947 Knucklehead that he tore apart over and over again from the time he bought it in 1963 until it took its final form, which is how it appears in this book. The only thing left of the old Knuck is the motor, which had been taken up to an unprecedented 100 cubic inches. That kind of

muscle joined with a Magnuson Supercharger and its array of belts and pulleys, the twin Weber carburetors, and the 5/8-inch Jim Davis chrome-moly frame set a new standard for innovation in custom bikes, not only for other builders but for Arlen himself. He called this his first "serious" bike. Since then, he has built many more serious bikes. When *Untouchable* debuted, it was painted blue, but the following year, 1977, having never been happy with the original color, Arlen repainted it red, saving the Dick DeBenedictis graphic that he loved.

Untouchable was the perfect bike to accompany Arlen on his first trip to Sturgis in 1976. It made quite the statement as Arlen rode it alongside Barry Cooney, who was riding his own digger, from their campsite in City Park to Main Street, which they cruised up and down before heading into Boulder Canyon for the ride to Deadwood. What a great place to meet new people and run into those he'd met over the last few years. The park was a particularly good place to be. Donnie Smith from Smith Brothers and Fetrow in Minneapolis was camped there, as was Arlin Fatland of 2-Wheelers in Denver. They rode, they drank, they partied, they talked bikes, and they became good friends. *Untouchable* went on to appear on the cover of the recently launched *Supercycle* magazine in 1977. For that cover photo, Bev dressed in gangster attire and posed beside the bike. Arlen's friend Larry Kumferman was hired to be the editor of *Supercycle*.

While Arlen's life and business was always getting better and better, the close of 1976 brought a tough personal turn for Arlen. Kevin relates, "Ervin got sick when he was in his late forties, early fifties. He had Parkinson's disease as well as atherosclerosis, and eventually he had a stroke. He died December 2." Ervin had been sick for some time, so his death wasn't completely unexpected, but it was a shock to get a call from the hospital

informing the family that Ervin was gravely ill. Arlen left immediately but his dad was already unconscious when he got to the room and he died shortly after. The torch had been passed; Arlen was now the Ness family patriarch.

Arlen still considered the Oakland Roadster Show held every January to be the show of shows. Having won the big trophy for his Knucklehead many years earlier, he had quit competing, but he always felt it was the best place to debut his new bikes. Every year, the Roadster Show was like a deadline for new builds. *Untouchable* was a huge hit at the 1976 show, but Arlen wanted something really different to ride into the exhibition hall for the 1977 show. His idea for a twin-engine Sportster materialized as *Two Bad,* which, to this day, is still one of Arlen's most unique and spectacular bikes.

It was an ambitious design, particularly with the show deadline. Johnny Lopez, who was now 23 and known to everyone as "Pretty Boy," was still working with Arlen in the garage and helped on much of the *Two Bad* project. In the years since Johnny started showing up at Arlen's as a teenager, he had become a fabricator in his own right. Larry Kumferman gave Johnny the nickname Pretty Boy after he heard a girl shout, "Who's the pretty boy in the garage?" and named one of Johnny's bikes in *Custom Bike Magazine Pretty Boy.*

With just two weeks left before the Roadster show, and *Two Bad* still quite a ways from completion, Barry Cooney arrived from Portland, Donnie Smith from Minneapolis, Dave Perewitz from Brockton, Massachusetts, Frances Dias from Hawaii,

Father-in-law Richard Rego Sr., Steve Desmond, Arlen, and his brother Kevin in the second store on 14th Street, San Leandro, California, c. 1982.
Ness Family archive

and Arlin Fatland came in from Denver. They arrived in San Leandro with plans to go riding at Arlen's invitation. As Donnie Smith recalls: "The plan was we were all going to get some bikes and ride up to Tahoe together. When we got out there, *Two Bad* wasn't finished so we

Arlen and Bev at a bike show, California, c. 1983.
Ness Family archive

decided we were all going to help Arlen work on it. We all crashed at the house. We were sleeping on couches and sleeping on the floor. Bev would make us food to eat. We would go out and work on this thing for 10 or 12 hours and then go out and drink. Arlen would stay back and work. We ended up having a really good time, and we got to know each other well. We were together for almost two full weeks. That's what made us gel together. Since then, we have all been really good friends."

Dave Perewitz was a little younger, and his only experience with tequila was the ride to Laconia with Arlen two years earlier. As he remembers, "I always partied as a kid, but when I went to California, those guys were serious drinkers. When they started on the tequila, they didn't stop."

Despite so many people working at the house, tequila must have diluted their collective memory because details are pretty sketchy today. They did get away to SO-CAL to an annual industry trade show the weekend before the Roadster show. For the trip, the group grew to one or two dozen, depending on who is telling the story. Kevin recounts: "We went down with a couple of limos in a convoy. I had a lowered silver Cadillac limo with wire wheels and tinted windows, and Arlen had a presidential stretch Lincoln that he bought sight-unseen out of *Hemmings Magazine*. He flew me and a friend back east to buy that car out of New York City not long before. It had a bad transmission in it, so he had the guy bring it to the nearest AAMCO shop to be fixed. We flew in, picked up the car, and drove up to Brockton to hang out with Perewitz. It was in pretty bad shape. Then we drove it through one of those dollar car washes and dented up the sides pretty bad because the car was so long. When we got to Dave's house, he helped us pound it back out. It was the middle of winter, so when we drove back, we hit a bunch of blizzards. Going through Wyoming, we bought some bullhorns for a hood ornament and toy pistols for the door handles. Arlen fixed it right up when we got back to California. He had it painted silver and charcoal."

They left San Leandro in a convoy. Kevin believes he had 11 people in the back of the limo he was driving. Arlen got Mike, the maitre d' from the nearby Farmers Restaurant, to take a few days off so he could drive his limo and serve drinks. Mike, like everyone else, was just there for the fun of it. Quite a few guys made the trip, but no one can really remember exactly who was there other than the guys working on the bike and Steve Allington, Bob Dron, and Tony Carlini. There are hazy recollections. Dave Perewitz was pushed out of the limo on Highway 5 to quickly purge the tequila he was just learning how to drink. Donnie Smith got carried up to his hotel room on Bob Dron's back when he couldn't walk, and the back seat in Kevin's limo caught fire from the heat of the exhaust pipes below it and had to be ripped out and hosed down. The rest has faded away.

The group was back in San Leandro early Monday morning to finish the bike. By Thursday, after several long days, it was ready. The 2,000-cc hand-fabricated beast was fired up. Replete with its Magnuson supercharger, four gas tanks, two Weber carburetors, center-hub steering, convoluted pipes, and countless other features, it was ridden into the show. A last minute add-on included a remote-control starter that Barry Cooney rigged up, which provided countless laughs as Arlen and his friends stood at a distance watching the shocked looks on the faces of the disbelieving spectators.

Just six weeks later was the annual Daytona BikeWeek, which Arlen had attended for the first time the previous year. This time around, now that all these builders were getting to know each other so well, they all showed up in Florida. On the East Coast, Susan Perewitz remembers, "Dave, Jimmy Leahy, and I drove down to Daytona together. There was a big blizzard on the way, and we couldn't wait to get there. We were riding, partying, hanging out, going booth to booth and bar to bar, all the things you do in Daytona. One afternoon, a couple of days after we got there, we went back to have a nap at the Mystic Sea Hotel, where we were all staying. When I got up, everyone was gone except me and Jimmy. We were left with no money, no food, no beer, nothing. So Jimmy started calling them all a bunch of 'F-ing Hamsters.' He drew hamsters on a bunch of paper plates we had in our room and wrote 'Hamster M/C' on each of them. Before putting them on everyone's door, he personalized them with 'Arlen Ness, West Coast Chapter President'; 'Dave Perewitz, East Coast

Chapter President'; and 'Donnie Smith, Midwest Chapter President' as a further dig. We just sat in the parking lot and waited for them to come back. When they finally came roaring in on their bikes, they went straight to their rooms, stopped, looked at the plates, and started laughing; they thought it was a riot. It was supposed to piss them off, and they just loved it. That whole week they called themselves the Hamsters. Jimmy went out and had a black shirt with white letters done up that said Hamsters M/C. Since then, we dropped the M/C; we are really just a group of motorcycle enthusiasts."

For the 1977 Daytona rally, Arlen rode *Two Bad* into the annual Harley-Davidson ride-in show and was awarded the first-place trophy, which was presented to him personally by Willie G. Davidson. That particular year, the trophy, from Cartier, was a unique handmade gold and silver replica of the original 1903 single-cylinder motorcycle built by Bill Harley and the Davidson brothers. It was supposedly valued in the $10,000 range, not your average bike-show trophy. It so impressed Arlen that when he got back to California, he was inspired to start working on an antique-themed custom that he later dubbed *Ness-tique.*

Ness-tique went to Sturgis the following year, in 1978, as Arlen's rider, even though, as Arlen says, "That thing is hard to ride. It was pretty flimsy and lightweight, but I could handle it pretty well. I rode all through Spearfish Canyon and all through the hills. I rode the shit out of it." When he ran into Willie G., he had that bike with him. More than a year had passed since Willie G. had awarded Arlen first-place in Daytona, and here was Arlen, with the very bike he built as a result of winning that trophy.

Arlen recalls, "It was getting dark as I pulled into Deadwood. There was a parking place in front of the No. 10 Saloon, so I pulled up and walked in. Willie G. was in there, so

Orange Luxury Liner is a great road bike. It was serial numbered as number one in a series of 50 Luxury Liners that were produced. The inspiration for these bikes came out of Arlen's personal riding experience, especially his cross-country group rides to Sturgis. He wanted to make a custom capable of long-distance travel yet one that still looked great. The rubber-mount Dyna-style frame was a good choice, making the bike an easy rider, and the stock 80-inch motor was a good choice for reliability. Carburetion is provided by an Edelbrock Quick Silver carb and braking provided by a Ness-PM setup with four-piston calipers. The saddlebags, fenders, and fairing are made of fiberglass but the gas tanks were hand formed from aluminum. The whole bike was loaded with Ness billet parts that could be ordered from the catalog. Arlen rode this bike to Sturgis when it was first built. Motorcycle enthusiast and *L.A. Times* newspaper owner Otis Chandler bought a similar Luxury Liner to ride, and it was also Chandler's bike that represented Arlen in the Guggenheim's "Art of the Motorcycle" exhibition when it opened in Las Vegas.

ALUMINUM OHC EVO

This all-aluminum bike features one of Arlen's early overhead-cam motors which he built from designs made expressly for him by Pete Ardema. It is very lightweight and easy to ride. Compared to stock frames which can weigh in at 40 pounds, this aluminum frame only weighs 17 pounds. Bob Munroe fabricated the oil tank, fuel tank, and fenders. The triple clamps, headlight, pipes, mufflers, and even the Evolution motor, with billet heads and barrels from Nigel Patrick of Patrick Racing, are all aluminum. The carb is from S&S and the tranny is an H-D Dyna Glide

rubber-mount. Wheels are aluminum alloy, 19-inch on front and 18-inch in the rear. One of the features that Arlen describes as "so cool" is the way these overhead-cam motors start without hardly turning over. With no inner valve springs, they also ride extra smooth and idle well. When the bike was debuted in Laughlin, no one had ever seen one before, so it generated a lot of excitement. Arlen enjoyed the bike so much that he rode it for a full year at all the major events.

OHC LUXURY LINER

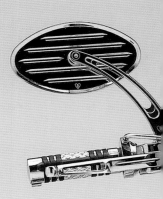

This green-and-white scalloped Luxury Liner is the only Luxury Liner that was built on a Softail frame. All of the others were built on Ness Dyna rubber-mount frames. It is also only one of two Luxury Liners that were built with the overhead-cam conversion. The 88-inch S&S motor is fitted with an S&S carburetor. Breaking comes from the standard issue Ness–Performance Machine brakes that are on all of Arlen's bikes by this time. The front end is made from 41-mm tubes with Ness lower legs and trees. By 1998, it was possible to build a bike like this, with the exception of the overhead-cam modification, from parts that could be ordered right out of the Ness catalog, but, of course, people want Arlen's bike. When he rode it to Sturgis in 1997, he let a number of friends try it and the response was incredible. Arlen had built a perfect bike for the trip; thanks to the overhead cams, it is extra smooth riding, starts instantly, and idles great. Arlen was offered top dollar for the bike but he won't let any of his OHC bikes go until they are commercially viable and available from him.

Arlen next to his
chopped, channeled, and
sectioned 1956
Ford pick-up, Brentwood,
California, 1987.

THE 1980S
AND THE BIG TIME

AS THE 1970s came to a close, it was clear that the 200-square-foot shop had served its purpose. Custom bikes had so grown in popularity that there really was an industry now to serve the growing demands. It was 1980 and time to step up to something more befitting of the growing business and reputation, yet it had to be done the way Arlen did everything else—conservatively, the way he knew would work for him. Arlen said, "We had grown out of the old space, so we bought a run-down building that was divided up in three little shops. It was an odd-shaped building and pretty run down. There were broken windows, and it was in sad shape, but we were able to fix it up by tearing down some walls and opening it up. Everything put together, it may have been 2,000 square feet. It was great to own our own building, and we knew we could afford it. We may have paid $75,000 for it."

Cory came into the business full-time right after graduating from high school in 1981, the year after they moved into the new store. He had been working in the shop and with Arlen for years, but now that he was out of high school he was ready for more responsibilities, and Arlen gave them to him. Cory needed to learn more about the business and about bikes, and he needed to make a name for himself. In the family tradition, he immediately started working on his own customs.

Arlen relates, "Cory built *Turned Loose* when he was just 19 and took it on the show circuit in 1981 and 1982. I pushed him to do that so he would talk to people, learn about traveling, and get good at it." The bike appeared on the cover of *Street Chopper* magazine with Cory's wife, Kim, in August, 1982. Cory was now on the way to developing his own reputation with the media and the public, just like his father had. But there was something missing this time around. Larry Kumferman, who had helped Arlen get into magazines and develop his reputation, was now gone. The close family friend was killed after the Sturgis rally in 1980 when a drunk driver jumped a stop sign and hit his trike.

Arlen continued traveling to events and shows all over the country. You could count on him appearing at Sturgis and Daytona each year. And he started visiting new events, particularly bike shows and swap meets. After the success of the factory-sponsored "Artistry in Iron" show in Los Angeles in 1980, the theme was taken to Calgary, Alberta, in 1983. The promoter brought Arlen in as a guest, but this was one show that wasn't meant to be.

Untouchable and an early front-sectioned Ness Sportster on display, Oakland Museum of California, 1987.

Arriving in Canada, Arlen remembers, "They kept me in immigration for over an hour. They kept me that long so they could check with every state to find something on me to keep me out, but there was nothing they could find. I didn't have any kind of record. The police didn't want the show to go on because they were afraid of what could happen with the bike clubs. By keeping me out, they thought that would hurt the show." Apparently, there were issues with a local bike club, and early that Saturday morning, the day the show was scheduled to open, a bomb went off, closing the venue down. I was at that show, too, and while we didn't get to see a bike show, Arlen, Steve Allington, Arlin Fatland, and I had a great time touring the mountains around nearby Banff.

This brings up something that's been an issue for many people in the bike business but not really for Arlen: how to deal with the clubs. Arlen simply says, "I always respected the clubs. They are just like anyone else. Just treat people like you want to be treated and do what you say you're going to do. Even now, when they have a poker run, I'll donate prizes,

but it's strictly business." He recalls, "Sonny [Barger] used to come into our second store a lot when he was building a bike for his wife that he wanted to show in the Oakland Roadster Show. I got him a lot of stuff, so he used some of our parts."

Year after year, Arlen's business grew despite what was going on in the world around. The biking boom of the 1970s was tapering off, as was the general economy. Problems were afoot for the industry. Harley-Davidson was itself going through many changes. In 1981, senior Harley executives bought the company back from AMF, but the company was struggling. Imports of large-displacement Japanese motorcycles made it increasingly difficult for H-D to compete in the marketplace, so in 1983, the company petitioned for tariff relief. They won their case, and a tariff scheduled to last five years was imposed on all Japanese motorcycle imports 700 cc or larger. The following year, the introduction of the Softail model

Arlen gets a kiss from his mother Elaine as he rides *Orange Blossom* into the Oakland Museum of California reception for the "California Dream" exhibit, Oakland, California, 1984.

Arlen and Cory in the second store on East 14th Street, San Leandro, California, 1987.

and the incredible 80-cubic-inch Evolution motor looked like it would bring the company to more solid footing, but there were deeper troubles. In 1985, with only seven days to secure financing before the company would be forced into bankruptcy, Harley's chief financial officer, Richard Teerlink, got last-minute loans and kept the assembly line running. It wasn't until 1986, when Harley went public with a listing on the American Stock Exchange, that its fortunes improved.

Arlen was aware of Harley's troubles but felt, "My business was so small that it didn't take much to keep me happy. I was still doing paint jobs and could live off that, so the recession had no effect on me." He now looks back and thinks, "If I knew then what I know now, thank god they didn't go out of business. There wouldn't be any custom or aftermarket business today." Arlen was in a better position

than some of his friends to weather the times. Barry Cooney got out in 1981 when things were still good to try some new things in San Diego. Less than two years after the sale, B.C. Choppers was out of business.

Donnie Smith stayed in for a few more years. Reflecting back on those times, Donnie said, "We went about five years doing almost three-hundred frames a year. It was like an assembly line. Then the recession and gas crunch came in. Everything slowed up and Fat Bob's took over. All those two-gallon-gas-tank bikes were finished. Everyone wanted four or five gallons of gas. That's when it all slowed up for everyone. One part of our business dropped eighty percent in one year. That's how fast the custom market changed. It was a good ride. We did it for fifteen years by the time we closed in 1985."

Arlin Fatland was also affected at his 2-Wheelers shop in Denver. Not only was he dealing with a bad economy, he had Harley hot on his tail. Many of the products he sold, like those at so many other shops, freely used the Harley-Davidson logo and trademarks. Harley didn't like the "free" part of "freely" and started to strictly enforce use of their trademark for the first time. Back in San Leandro, Arlen wasn't dependent on the Harley logo. He may have used the number "1" trademark or elements that resembled pieces of the logo at that time, but he says, "I just got rid of every possible resemblance from that point on. I didn't want to be associated with them and haven't worn anything with the Harley logo on it since." His own brand identity was developing, which could insulate him from the economic dips and dives and industry trends that so affected other shops.

Other factors may have affected how Arlen felt about the factory. It was around the same time, after the Evolution motor was released in 1983, that he had another encounter with Harley. "The new Evolution had rubber mounts on the heads to which the carburetor was attached. Those things failed immediately. They wouldn't hold up, they'd just crack and suck air. It was a huge warranty problem for the dealers. so I made aluminum castings to replace the rubber mount.

"Then I supplied an O-ring that would go onto the stock manifold and then slip inside the casting that I made. I called it the 'Evolution Solution' and got a patent pending on it. Harley invited me to San Francisco to have a meeting with me on my design to consider carrying it. I brought them a sample and showed them some other parts I had with me. They took my stuff with them, and I heard they tested and tested it. One of the engineers told me six months later that the Evolution Solution worked fine, but they never did do anything with it. Unfortunately, I didn't have patents on the other parts, and sure enough, they copied them overseas."

Despite heeding the advice Gary Bang gave years before, Arlen's designs were copied by many companies. He did his best to avoid having his designs copied by staying ahead of the curve, but it was a fact of

Arlen and Sherri at a family gathering.
Ness Family archive

business. As his old friend Jack Luna explained, "Arlen was always coming up with a better mousetrap. He always put a different spin on things. The 1980s were when they came out with the FXRs, which were so popular. He did a lot to modify them. He came out with different fairings, side covers, wheels, and other parts. As they came out with new models of motorcycles, Arlen was there to modify them and make them custom. He was always a step ahead. By the time they came out with something, he would have something to make them look better."

Others in the industry were scrambling to stay afloat, but Arlen was seemingly in his own world, doing his own thing. You can imagine his surprise when the Oakland Museum of California called and asked if they could include Arlen in a permanent exhibit they were installing called "California Dream." Arlen explains that the theme focused on "why people come to California, so they had old movie cameras from Hollywood, a custom car from Barris, and they bought an orange diamond-tank Sportster from me. I also loaned them *Untouchable,* which they had on display for ten years. They came to me, so

Cory riding one of his early customs with Arlen, who rides the *Blower Bike*, California, c. 1988. *Ness Family archive*

I always thought that was a feather in my cap, to have a permanent display in a museum. For the reception, they had me ride *Orange Blossom* right into the middle of the reception with all the noise. There was quite a crowd of people that donate to the museum, and my mom was there. She was very proud."

The reception, which was held in November, 1984, also celebrated the 15th anniversary of the museum. So thousands of people who were in the museum for the anniversary were wondering where the noise was coming from. Steve Allington was there, along with Arlen's family and other friends like Jeff McCann, Johnny Lopez, and Jim Davis. Steve remembers, "I was in awe that a local motorcycle guy that I rode with and once saw get turned away from a gas pump because they didn't serve 'our kind' had the prestigious Oakland Museum looking at him as an artist. To me, this was the turning point at which our society starting to see us as real people."

As Harley-Davidson teetered on the edge of bankruptcy in 1985, Arlen took to the air with Arlin Fatland and Steve Allington to see what kind of business opportunities were available in the Pacific Rim. It was the first passport any of them had ever had. Fortunately, Joe Phillipson, a motorcycle parts importer who had planned the trip for them, knew the program. He met them at the airport in Taiwan, made sure they made it to the aftermarket parts trade show they were there for, got them around town, and showed them some of the sights. As far as the traveling trio was concerned, it was all new and different. Steve says, "It was like a parade all around us with whole families on Vespas."

Arlin Fatland recalls, "They were selling ducks and geese and snakes and alcohol, and liquids we had no idea what they were. They've got these ducks and geese hanging from their tents. It was really weird. Then some guys came by that cut the heads off snakes, turned them upside down, and held their bodies up to their mouths to suck out the blood. I have no idea what they were doing. It was crazy and something you sure wouldn't see back home!"

Despite the distractions, they did make the business connections they went to make. Arlen placed an order for several parts right away, and in the years that followed he had many of his own parts made there. Now, 20 years later, he is still getting great quality product from the same manufacturer he connected with on that trip.

By 1986, Cory fully understood Arlen's business. Having been raised with custom bikes being built at the house every day, knowing the people, going to shows, and

Arlen in the showroom
of his second
San Leandro store,
with *Two Bad* in the
background, 1987.

hanging around the shop, he understood the
business in a way no one else could. Anything
he didn't learn that way, he learned working
beside Arlen the last few years and on his
own. Cory was ready to take over more of the
daily duties, venture into new areas they
hadn't yet explored, and turn Arlen Ness, Inc.,
into a business that he was just starting to
envision. Convinced that the best opportunity
for growth was in the catalog, that year he
took full responsibility for producing it, including organizing products, writing copy,
arranging photography, and handling the
printing. He felt it was the one area where he
could reach out and target the bigger market
that appreciated Arlen's bikes and talent.

   With Cory being more active, it was
easier for Arlen to get away and devote more
time to working on project bikes back at the
house. He also had more time to travel to the
increasing number of shows and events, and
he had some time for personal travel. Now
that he had a passport and had taken one
overseas trip, Arlen was ready to see more of
the world. Tony Carlini, who had become
a close friend over the years, especially since
his move from Detroit to Southern California,
proposed a great trip to Italy. He wanted t
o look at a rare Ferrari he was interested in
buying. His uncle, Hank Carlini, Lee Iacocca's
right-hand man, had been living in Torino, Italy,
working on the Pantera program. He had
connections and made arrangements for Arlen
and Tony to get the royal treatment at the
Ferrari factory in Modena; the De Tomaso
factory, where they made the Pantera, also in
Modena; and the Lamborghini factory in the
small village of Sant'Agata Bolognese. They
even went to some high-powered dinners with
Hank and sports car execs involved with the
Chrysler buyout of Lamborghini, which was
taking place at that time.

   Arlen recalls trip highlights, which include
going for a test drive in the experimental

Arlen and Bev in front of their Castro Valley home with the 1977 Ford Van, 1972 Rolls Royce Cornich convertible, and the 1956 Ford pickup in the garage, 1987.

Lamborghini LM-series Hummer-style truck. "A famous test driver took us for a test ride at over 100 mph on those small back roads where you can come up on a hay wagon. I was holding on as tight as I could as we slid around corners. Those guys have no fear. It was quite an experience." They also got insight into the Italians' painting methods. "We got to go inside the paint booth, which was neat, since both of us were painters. It was interesting that the base coats on their reds were actually a bright yellow."

After returning from that trip, Arlen bought his first Ferrari. It was a 206 he got from Hank. What Arlen really wanted was the far more expensive Testarossa. Ideas were brewing. Arlen sold the 206 to buy a 308GTB, picked it up, and drove it straight to Boyd Coddington's shop, where Craig Naff was ready to start work. They were going to turn the 308GTB into something closer to the Testarossa. Arlen wasn't interested in building a replica either; he had every intention of improving it, especially since he never liked the back end of the

stock factory car. He planned to make his car wider and longer and basically cooler overall. A wizard with steel, Craig was the one who could make this happen.

In the process of working on the car, plans were put into motion to make an accompanying custom bike. The bike was to also have the look of a Testarossa with the help of molded aluminum body panels. For the first time ever, Arlen had drawings made to help envision the bike. This was before the days of fat-tire bikes, so a car rim and tire were adapted for the purpose. When complete, Arlen recalls, "It handled terribly. I could ride it, and I rode it quite a bit, but it didn't handle worth a shit with that car tire. The bike has so much stuff on it that it's a very heavy bike. It was ahead of its time." He even ground the edges of the tire with a grinder, which didn't help. "I rode it 300 miles to the Redwoods in one day, and it just about wore me out. I remember getting to the hotel and flopping on the bed," Arlen said. *Ferrari Bike* was a two-year project from drawings to

street. Arlen debuted it in Sturgis, where he rode it in August of 1989, but it was still in raw metal. It wasn't until the following January that people finally saw it at the Oakland Roadster Show replete with its many coats of Ferrari red paint.

During the time *Ferrari Bike* was being built, changes were afoot at the store. Arlen's confidence in Cory was paying off. Not even 25, Cory was hitting the nail on the head. Catalog sales were taking off and driving the business. By 1988, the space they purchased only eight years earlier, thinking it would last forever, wasn't big enough for all their parts or their workforce, now numbering 10. Arlen was also amassing a collection of his own bikes that needed to go somewhere. He wanted to put them on display in a museum setting. After searching for something that would work, Arlen says, "We bought another place on East 14th Street and moved into 5,000

square feet of it right away. There were a bunch of little buildings on the property, and the guy I bought it from rented part of it back for a year, which helped us out. When he moved out and we took that over, we ended up with 15,000 square feet." While it took about a year from the time they moved in, Arlen made a space at the new shop for his bikes. "I had to raise the ceiling in the attic and level the floors to make the museum. You had to ask us and get escorted through the warehouse to get up there. Once people heard about it, they came from everywhere to see the bikes."

With the move to the new store, the growth, and increased catalog sales, it was time to revisit computerizing their business accounting. A couple of years earlier, Bev showed me an IBM PC computer that her neighbor Jerry Ferreira had given them. It was in a closet collecting dust, because she

Arlen driving his 1977 chopped, channeled, and sectioned Ford van, California, 1987.

was never able to get it working properly. Now she realized that computerization was an absolute necessity. Jerry, who ran his own accounting business, came in five days a week until the transition was complete. His assistant, Meg Humphries, helped on the project, and to this day, they are both still working in their I.T. department. Jerry comes in just a couple of days a week, but Meg now works there full-time.

In those last few years of the 1980s, in addition to *Ferrari Bike*, other serious bikes like *Accel* and *Blower Bike* rolled out of Arlen's shop. He had made a conscious decision "to step it up and do more radical stuff. It may have had something to do with having more time now that Cory was so involved." As he always knew, the serious bikes were great at shows and made a difference in the extra publicity they generated.

Unfortunately, *Ferrari Bike* would be Jim Davis' last project with Arlen. He had made all Arlen's frames since the day Arlen walked into his shop almost 20 years before. Jim was heavily into biking, which is understandable. As a drag racer, he loved speed, and the bikes he built went fast. He looked forward to Sturgis every year for the riding, to catch up with the many biking friends he now had, and to party. He built a 40-foot trailer and would

usually take a load of friend's bikes to Denver, where they would all meet at Arlin Fatland's for a big pre-Sturgis party and then ride up to the Black Hills. Despite Arlen's traveling, busy schedule, and rise to fame in the bike world, the two men still got together twice a week to talk about new projects or the frames. Arlen would go out to Jim's house to pick up some parts or drop something off at the shop, and invariably they would go out to eat or have a drink. This all came to an unexpected end on February 16, 1989, when Arlen was at the annual Cincinnati Powersports Show. "I remember getting the phone call at my hotel. I was in shock. They told me Jim was killed in a wreck on his motorcycle. A flatbed semi without any lights on the trailer backed out onto a small, dark country road out in Brentwood where he lived. He was on his way home with his wife, Carol. Jim hit the trailer and was killed. His wife, Carol, was in critical condition but survived."

After Jim died, Arlen started to ride straight from California to Sturgis with Barry Cooney. It was just the two of them at first, but each year, more friends would join them. Eventually, it turned into the annual "Sturgis Hamster Ride," with well over 100 bikes snaking their way along a different route to the rally each year. That fun little group of builders in Daytona in 1977 had grown. By the early 1990s, it had become a much larger group of enthusiasts, tied together by their love of custom bikes. They had quite the presence in Sturgis, especially when they rode down Main Street on Thursday for their annual ride-through. You were supposed to have put your own bike together to be in the Hamsters, but some members had clearly paid for high-dollar builds. Then again, their one rule was "there are no rules," and the Hamsters were really just about having a lot of fun.

RED ROCKET

This bike clearly sprouts from high-performance drag racing roots. Powered by an S&S 100-inch motor that Arlen reconfigured as an overhead cam, it can deliver. It was fed by an S&S carb and was followed by an FXR five-speed tranny. The FXR frame was modified by drastically changing the shock angle to lower the seating position. With so little room under the seat, the battery was moved forward into the large front spoiler. Now that 330 and 360 rear tires are available, we take for granted that it wasn't long ago that there wasn't anything over a 180. For *Red Rocket*, Arlen had to weld two rims together to make one wide enough for the recently released Avon 200x18 rear tire. The wheel was mounted in a special double rail

swingarm that added strength and further strengthened the drag racing connection. A drive-side brake and 15-inch pulley combo was unusual for the time, as was the six-piston rear caliper. The short, stubby front end was made to look even shorter by the 21-inch wheel and has an almost busy appearance with the dual 13-inch rotors and twin Ness-PM six-piston calipers. The long and swoopy fuel tank was another thing that has become common in recent years but was very different in 1998.

AVON BIKE

Arlen set out to make a short and fat performance style bike as he put together plans for *Avon Bike*. The one-off rigid frame was fabricated in-house to accommodate the recently released 230x15 Avon rear tire, the widest tire available at the time. A big front tire adds to the bike's stubby appearance. Because this bike was made as part of Arlen's long-standing relationship with Avon, the tire company used it in some of their ads. Arlen also used the tire connection as an opportunity to revive the tread-pattern paint motif that he used on fenders ten years earlier. Danny Gray stitched together another fitting seat, just as he always does. The motor for this fast-looking bike is a 100-inch S&S big twin with an S&S carburetor. While there is no speedo to track his speed, Arlen has a tach prominently mounted front and center on the handlebars. The bike debuted in Sturgis, which was the perfect place to put it through its paces.

NESS COUNTY FIRE ENGINE BIKE

Fire Engine Bike is similar to *Avon Bike.* It is based on the same custom-made rigid frame supporting an Avon 230 rear tire, uses a 100-inch S&S motor, an S&S carburetor, and also has the large tachometer mounted high on the handlebars. The fire engine theme was picked because it was a great theme—this was two full years before 9/11 and the many fire-theme tribute bikes that followed that tragic event. As for style, Arlen set out to make a bagger drag bike with a pro street look. There is a super charger on the left side and a nitrous bottle next to the rear cylinder, which looks like it is ready for a fireman to grab so he can race into a

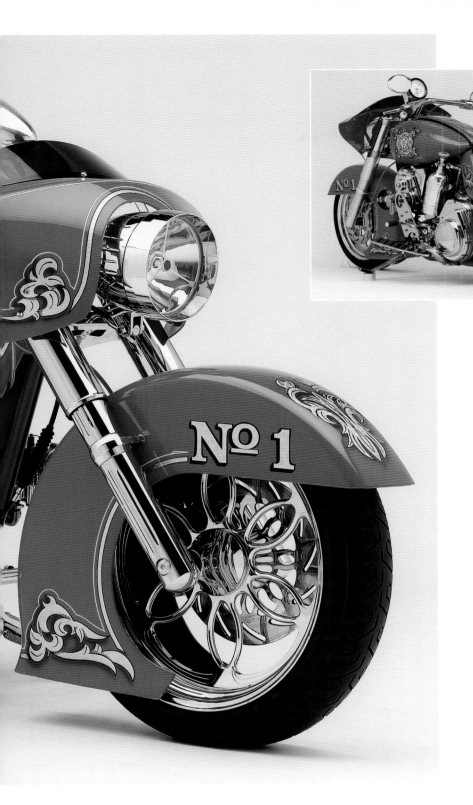

burning building. There was a lot of surface area for Steve Farone to paint his amazing details. The rear-section one-piece body includes a very enlarged fender that drapes over the sides of the bike into the Luxury Liner–style saddlebags and forward into the faux fire engine side panels. The gas tanks were also encased in a fiberglass cover that flows down right into a lower fairing. Once again, Arlen tied his name into the name of the bike—it appears in the wonderful Ness County emblem on the sides of the tanks.

VICTORY LUXURY LINER

Arlen made this bike before he had a working relationship with Victory.
Victory provided him with the motor, tranny, and frame and he came up with the rest. He first modified the stock Victory frame by stretching the swingarm, lowering the seat position by relocating the shock, and then doing a front section to add a five-inch front stretch. The gas tank started as standard steel fat bob tanks that Bob Munroe stretched in back. Bob also hand fabricated the aluminum side covers. The fairing, Luxury Liner saddlebags, and fenders are all from fiberglass and were available right out of the Ness catalog. Arlen added frame covers to cover the down tubes and to hide

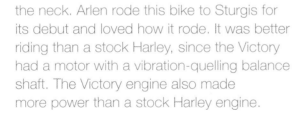

the neck. Arlen rode this bike to Sturgis for its debut and loved how it rode. It was better riding than a stock Harley, since the Victory had a motor with a vibration-quelling balance shaft. The Victory engine also made more power than a stock Harley engine.

ARROW BIKE

Like *Smooth-Ness*, the idea for *Arrow Bike* came from an early car. There wasn't a specific car, but Arlen recalls art deco–looking open-fendered cars from the 1920s and 1930s. The chassis was another one of his special-production rubber-mount Softail frames with shocks underneath the stock FXR transmission. Like many of his frames, this bike also uses a five-inch stretch and 38-degree rake configuration. The bike is powered by a stock 80-inch Evolution motor. Bob Munroe hand made the pipes with a big radius and did all of the aluminum work, hand forming the gas tank, front fender, and back fender, which flowed right into the side panels that encased the battery and oil tank. Taillights were flush mounted into the elongated back fender and a custom Danny Gray seat fit right into the bodywork. The 200x18 back and 21-inch front Avon tires were mounted on Akron rims that were laced in-house. This elegant bike was another opportunity for Arlen to tie his passion for cars and bikes together.

Arlen's custom bikes on display outside his third East 14th Street store, San Leandro, California, 1989.

Group photo of the Hamsters in front of the Cottonwood Lodge in Spearfish, South Dakota, during Bike Week in the Black Hills, 1996.

and with Connie on the back, I didn't feel very comfortable riding it. Arlen offered to trade with me. I didn't know it at the time, but he was just recovering from a broken leg and was still limping yet he went right ahead and took that full dresser. It was amazing."

Bev, as it turns out, loved riding on the back of the dresser, something she had never done before! She recalls the trip: "The countryside and places we stayed were breathtaking. Some things were like picture postcards. Stopping for the cows with the great big bells around their necks—they had

the right of way. You see so much more on a bike. Maybe you pay more attention. The camaraderie was a great part of it with all the laughing because we were there to have a good time. Arlen's name was known, but it never got in the way. After the first day, everyone felt at ease and realized he doesn't have any arrogance and he's just a regular guy. The next year they asked us back to go to Spain, and then in 1995 we went to Italy."

HALF & HALF

***Half and Half* developed from a modified version of Arlen's Antique Kit which was designed for Sportsters.** While he had purchased the rights to the kit back in 1994, it appeared in the Ness catalog for the first time in 2005. In the time between, the bikes were mostly built by Arlen himself and by some of his builder friends like Dave Perewitz, Danny Gray, Don Hotop, and Fred Cuba. For this particular bike, Arlen chose a Shovelhead motor that he felt had an older look. The primary and tranny came from a stock H-D FXR.

The orange-black and black-orange inverse paint scheme was something he did just for fun. It was well received as he rode it around Sturgis and Daytona in 1999. Arlen likes the look of these antique kit bikes so much that he keeps one mounted high up in his living room at home. The real fun is that they are so light and nimble to ride, you can zip around quickly on them. He recently took *Half and Half* to a rally in Tennessee where he quickly smoked the tire in the burn-out pit.

NESS PATROL

"Safety and Service"

Ness Patrol* is Arlen's second police-theme bike and one of a series of theme bikes that Arlen came out with in the late 1990s, including *Ness Taxi* and *Ness County Fire Engine Bike.
The bikes were usually built on Softail platforms in a bagger style so there were more surfaces for paint. This frame was actually an early prototype Softail frame he had lying around. A stock Harley 80-inch Evo motor was used in conjunction with a Jim's six-speed transmission. The aluminum gas tank was stretched and narrowed by Bob Munroe who also made the side panels. the 200 rear tire is mostly hidden by the bodywork. On the front end are early perimeter brakes and high intensity beams from a car. While the overall look of the bike was similar to the earlier Luxury Liners, Arlen has taken the look to the next level. The fairing and tail-dragging fenders have gone through extensive glass modifications as have the saddlebags, which were stretched. Steve Farone did the exceptional paint and Danny Gray made the seat. Arlen enjoyed riding this bike enough to take it on Kyle Petty's "Ride Across America" as well as to Sturgis.

BIG-NESS/LITTLE-NESS

BIG-NESS/LITTLE-NESS

Arlen decided to make an overhead-cam version of Harley's "B" twin-cam motor after it was first released and it seemed to have a problem with timing chains breaking. The overhead cam was Arlen's solution to their problem. He used the stock H-D tranny but decided to bore the motor out to 95-inches. He chose a stock Ness Softail frame for the platform. Other features include a 21-inch front wheel with perimeter Ness-PM brakes and a 200x18 rear tire. The bike is loaded with

Ness billet parts and catalog parts like the stock front end, long fenders, and some of the first "Slasher" pipes that they made. While Arlen was already involved with this build, Ridley approached him about taking one of their small bikes and customizing it. The idea came to Arlen that it would be great to do them as a matching pair; the big one for himself and the small one for his oldest grandson, Zach, who was eleven at the time. The overhead cam is still the only Harley twin cam motor he has used for a custom.

DOUBLE OHC EVO

This bike has the only double-overhead-cam Evo motor that Arlen has ever heard of. Pete Ardema, who Arlen works with on all of the overhead cams, did the conversion of the S&S 100-inch motor. Arlen prefers to think of the modification as an overhead four cam because it has a cam for each valve. Even though this bike looks like a Softail and started life that way, it has been converted to a rubber-mount Dyna frame with shocks added in the back. Other notable features include the early use of a drive-side pulley-rotor combo and the twin perimeter front brakes that Arlen continued to experiment with. Bob Munroe built up and stretched the steel gas tank so it plunged back into the Danny Gray seat, and Carl Brouhard was brought on board to do the multi-colored paint job. Any parts that weren't custom made for the bike came from the Ness catalog. While Arlen has never sold an overhead cam motor, it is not something he has forgotten about. He loves everything about them from the way they run to their mechanical looks. People always ask about them and the overhead cam remains a big project on the back burner that will hopefully become commercially viable in the future.

SCREAMIN' NESS-ESSITY

With as many bikes as Arlen builds and keeps, it is no wonder he doesn't get to ride any one bike for very long. *Screamin' Ness-essity* is an exception. Arlen likes this bike so much that he has ridden it to Sturgis for four consecutive years and he plans to keep riding it. The bike seems a natural development from the earlier Luxury Liners, taking them to the next level. Built on a heavily modified stock

H-D FXR frame, Arlen dropped the seat position and stretched it front and back. It has a 107-inch balanced-shaft motor with a rubber-mounted Baker six-speed transmission. The brakes and calipers, including the perimeter brakes on the 21-inch front wheel, are from Ness. Features like the stretched saddlebags, low seating, good horsepower, and the nine-gallon fuel tank made by Bob Munroe make this road bike

the perfect highway cruiser. Geared high with a 65-tooth rear pulley, the engine only turns 2,700 rpm's at 80 miles per hour. Steve Farone finished the bike with a beautiful eagle-theme paint job. This bike generates many requests from people who would be interested in buying something similar. Unfortunately, custom baggers are slow and expensive to make. This idea may still be a few years out.

LUXURY LINERS, OVERHEAD CAMS, AND BREAKING GROUND

DURING 1993 and 1994, as Arlen worked on *Ness-Stalgia* and *Smooth-Ness*, he became aware of a unique antique-looking bike that Ron Russell had developed in Salinas utilizing an Ironhead Sportster motor. Arlen thought it had a great look. "Ron tried to make a business out of the bike, but it wasn't working, so I bought what he had: a trailer with some jigs, a couple of frames, and a sidecar. It just sat in my warehouse for a couple of years before I got around to building the first one." As it came to him, the bike had a permanently mounted sidecar in which the gas tank was mounted, while the oil was located where the gas would normally be. Of course, Arlen wanted to make changes before making the first one with his name on it. The main modification was to allow the bike to work without the sidecar by putting the fluids back where they would normally be. That first antique-style build, which he painted a solid red, was well received. Other modifications followed, which allowed the bikes to be powered by modern Sportster motors and even big-block Evos.

All the long-distance riding Arlen was doing at that time got him thinking about how to make this type of riding better. The custom bagger *Bat Bike* still worked well, but he wanted to take the approach to the next level.

Arlen bought a used stock police bike, modified the frame to make it longer and lower, added aluminum saddlebags, and painted it yellow for the next trip to Sturgis. A lot of the guys riding with him loved what Arlen was doing with these custom baggers. This particular one worked so well that Arlen shipped it to Spain for his second Edelweiss tour in 1994 and then left it in Europe with Ricky Battastini so he could ride it the following year through Italy. The yellow bike more or less became a model for a series of custom baggers that Arlen called Luxury Liners.

Orange Luxury Liner, the first of the series, was ready for the 1996 Sturgis rally. Arlen recounts, "I knew it was going to be a great road bike. It was long and low with a modified fairing and saddlebags and was built on a Ness Dyna Glide–style frame. There were long running boards on it so you can move your feet around, because they are so comfortable. Any time I had a chance, I would let friends try it. They were instantly hooked because of how smooth and easy it was to ride. It was also like having two bikes in one. Once you got there, you took off the bags, and the mounts that were bolted to the fender rails. It wasn't like a bagger without bags. Those look horrible. It looked more like a street hot rod." The Luxury Liners became

Arlen's first production bikes. Each was painted differently and may have had minor differences, but they were serial-numbered as part of a series.

The mid-1990s was a very busy period for Arlen, with projects like the Luxury Liners, the antique-style bikes, theme bikes, body bikes, and, of course, the overall business, which was continually growing. In anticipation of further growth, Arlen bought land to the east, over the hill in the town of Dublin. It was looking as if he'd need it some day. Arlen, in typical fashion, saw everything around him as a source for leads, inspiration, and ideas. His bikes seemed to be getting bigger and more stylized, but he never forgot his interest in performance and technology.

Arlen remembers, "Bill Davis, one of the guys who took phone orders in the store, was at a hot rod show in Pleasanton, and Pete Ardema was there with an overhead-cam motor on a Chevy. Pete said he wanted to try one on a motorcycle, so Bill wrote down his name and number and brought it back. I got in touch with him and we worked something out. I sent him all the parts he would need to get started and paid for the R&D until we got it going. Then Pete made us some kits to test. I bolted one onto a stock bagger that Cory bought. He rode it to Sturgis, and it worked great all the way there. Then the next year, I put one on a green-and-white Softail version of the Luxury Liner and I rode it to

Sturgis. I thought the overhead cam was great, because you don't have inner valve springs and that makes the bike turn over a lot easier. The motor revs free and is happy without all that spring pressure. Everybody was amazed when they saw it. It gave us more credibility, always coming out with cutting-edge stuff like that. Not only did we go for cosmetics, we were also working to improve performance."

Arlen went on to hire Nick Nichols to do some real-world testing of the motor. As an "Iron-Butt" rider and motorcycle product tester with more than one-and-a-half million logged miles, he was the person who could put the motor through its paces. Nick explains, "I ride one of every kind of bike because I work for all of the companies, but my primary bike is a Harley dresser. In 1998, I put an overhead cam in my 1986 FXRD bagger when Arlen and Cory sent me the motor. I put 50,000 miles on it riding all over the United States. At one point, I rode the bike from Texas back to Arlen's in California, and Jeff Borders worked with me in the shop to make some changes to the cams, nothing major. Then I went back out on the road,

Arlen on the *Gibson Bike* in Sturgis, South Dakota, 2003.

and it ran great once we found that happy medium. We weren't out to make a race motor out of it. We just wanted something dependable that anybody could get on and ride, and that's what we came to. It would make an excellent motor for anyone, and I think there is a very good future in it. The cam, the pushrods, the lifters, all that wasted motion is eliminated. It starts quick in any kind of weather and can be more efficient than a push-rod motor. It is the wave of the future. All the other motorcycle companies have already found that out except for Harley. I would like to see Arlen and Cory do it right now, but they just have too many projects going. If they came out with the overhead cam, I would put it in my own bike, without a doubt. We need to get it out on the road again."

Arlen has always loved trying different ideas and working in different styles, but the overhead cam may be the most technologically rooted of all of them. He went on to put it into quite a few machines, like his *Aluminum Overhead Cam* and *Double Overhead Cam* Evo, but has never sold any of them. Arlen explains, "We have a lot of money in the overhead cam. It has been a huge undertaking, but I know it works. It is always in the back of our minds to come back to it. Maybe that will be as a joint venture with another company some day." Hopefully, it won't be too far in the future.

Large double-decker rigs became popular on the motorcycle circuit in the late 1990s, but the trend dated back to the 1980s when Harley-Davidson had their big trucks crisscrossing the country. Then in 1989, Custom Chrome became the first after-market company to get involved when they purchased their big rig. Dan Stern, the vice president at Custom Chrome who originally proposed the program, explains, "That first truck was all black with a walk-through display. We ran it for two years, and it did about 36 events that first year. We were running the wheels off it. Then we realized people didn't want to go inside a truck and we needed more room and comfort, so we got the white truck, which had a cab that was like a motor home. It was real high-tech at the time, a double-decker with roll-out displays so that everything occurred outside of the truck. When we bought it, that truck and trailer cost about $650,000, not counting the displays."

After running the second truck for five years, Custom Chrome sold it to American Image, a company that manufactured Harley-Davidson clones for a short time. Prior to the sale Custom Chrome was spending close to $400,000 a year to keep the rig staffed and rolling to all the shows. It wasn't long before Arlen heard that the new owners were running into trouble. The driver of American Image's rig, Charlie Bryant, recalls, "Arlen came over to look at the truck and wanted to buy it. He asked me if I'd come with it and said he wouldn't buy the truck if I didn't take the job. I was actually retired already and just driving the truck part time, but I decided to take the job.

"We tried to break even with the truck by doing sales of parts, clothing, and bikes out of it, but it's so expensive to run the trucks. Those guys want anywhere from $3,000 to $20,000 to park a semi for a week plus getting it there and paying the staff. That's pretty tough to break even. Last year, I was on the road 220 days, most of them with my wife, Betty, and my dog, Spanky." Charlie's original plan was not to drive that many days or keep the job for very long, but once he got on the road and experienced how he was treated as part of the Ness family, he kept on driving.

Steve Farone working on a set of Ness tanks, Hayward, California, 2004.

Thinking back to the fateful day, April 4, 1999, Bev relates, "I was shocked. They thought I was fine until the reports came back. Then Arlen broke down a few times. Here's this positive guy, and he thought, 'You are just going to have to get better.' He was beside himself and had a real hard time being the quiet guy he is and keeping it inside. It's a personal thing to him, and he's not a guy who can talk to everybody. With me he tried to have a stiff upper lip, but there were times he was just himself and we both cried. It was probably the hardest thing we have ever dealt with." For the first year after the diagnosis and through the treatment phase, the illness occupied much of their days. Cancer is so prevalent in our society that reminders seem to be all around us. Fortunately, Bev responded positively to the treatments and has been cancer-free ever since.

Arlen riding *Avon Bike* during its debut in Sturgis, South Dakota, 1999.

A highlight of his time on the truck was a trip to Puerto Rico that he describes as "a truck driver's dream to put your rig on a boat and take it to another place." While Charlie finally retired in 2005 after seven years, the Arlen Ness semi continues to tour and make quite a splash wherever they set up.

As the new millennium approached, some people imagined new beginnings while others were certain about computers crashing and technology failures. The Ness family had much greater concerns. "Bev was in the hospital for an operation, and they thought everything was going to be OK," Arlen recounts. "When the doctor came in the next day for his rounds, he told her she had stage-three colon cancer, and I wasn't there. He didn't have very good bedside manners. Who knows why he didn't wait to tell her until I got back. When I returned a couple of hours later, Bev told me what the doctor said. It didn't register right away, because I didn't really understand it. I remember talking to the doctor right after, and that's when I realized how serious it was. We called Juris Bunkis, a real-good doctor friend that rides bikes I've built for him, and he steered us in the right direction. Bev is a trooper and got through it real well. Five years is supposed to be the magic time, but it's still scary. She is the main thing in my life, and the thought of losing her is too much."

The beginning of the new millennium did bring something new for Arlen, a formal relationship with Victory Motorcycles. Arlen and Cory signed the agreement in 2001, outlining a working relationship in which the two would both act as design consultants. They've each given their input to Victory's design department and have made two to three trips a year to have face-to-face meetings and review the latest designs. Victory then proceeded to market an Arlen Ness Signature Kingpin model and a Cory Ness Signature Vegas model, and both Arlen and Cory have appeared in Victory promotions. Arlen has also built three concept bikes on the Victory platform.

Arlen says, "I enjoy working on the Victory, too. They lend themselves to customizing real well, and because they are unit constructed, they are faster to put together."

The same year the Victory deal came together, Arlen had a personal tragedy on July 29, 2001, the day before leaving for Sturgis. Arlen explains, "Everybody was in town getting ready to leave for Sturgis the next morning. I was out visiting my mom, who was in an assisted-living home in San Leandro. My brother, Kevin, just happened to be there, too. She died peacefully while we were both at her bedside." Elaine had a big impact on Arlen. She was very sharp, talented, and creative. Kevin believes that these traits in Arlen came right from her.

In 2002, an opportunity arose when it looked like the Indian Motorcycle dealer in Daytona Beach was having difficulties. Bruce Rossmeyer, the owner of the Daytona Harley-Davidson dealership, as well as quite a few others, made an offer on that store and on the Miami dealership owned by the same people. Then Bruce proposed that they turn it into an "Arlen Ness Custom Motorcycles" store, reviving the concept Arlen had tried 30 years earlier.

Arlen explains, "Cory and I had become friends with Bruce. I built him some bikes to sell in his main store. Bruce bought both dealerships with the idea that we could go in on it as partners to sell our products. We always wanted to build motorcycles, so if that happens, it will be a great outlet. We knew Bruce and his staff, with their experience, can run it. Bruce wanted to give Shelly a shot at it. She had been working in the finance department at the dealership and he was confident she could do a great job. It has worked out well. Shelly is a chip off the old block, and sales the last couple of years have been great. We are number-one in sales of American

Arlen on his custom Victory motorcycle, Daytona Beach, Florida, 2001.

Ironhorse, and they are number two." It was decided to not renew the Miami lease when it expired after the first year and instead focus their energies in Daytona.

A new store will open in Las Vegas, Nevada, a great city for displaying Arlen's wares. The partner in this new venture is Arnie Araujo, an old friend and riding buddy of Arlen's. As happens so often, Arlen's business and personal relationships seem to blend together. Arnie recalls just how far back they go: "I used to own the Piccadilly Bar in Castro Valley, California, when long stretched Sportsters were really in. They all used to come to the bar, and we'd call them the 'Harley Boys.' That's when I first heard of Arlen. I went for a ride with them in 1976 and my wife, Larue, said, 'We've got to have one of them.'" Soon after, the couple did own their own Arlen Ness bike and went on to buy several more.

The land purchased in Dublin had been vacant since 1995, and the need for a new store kept growing. Bert Hamrel, a contractor and good friend of Arlen's, was instrumental in helping with the initial design and in moving the project forward. Arlen Ness Enterprises finally broke ground in 2000 when the land was graded and piers poured. They originally planned to build a 40,000 square foot building on a single floor. After running into some snags, construction was halted as a new architect and contractor (Bert's bigger projects were taking too much of his time) were brought on board. Once construction resumed on a greatly expanded building in the fall of 2002, work proceeded quickly. Sixteen months later, on March 29, 2003, they were ready for the grand opening of the new store, which was now almost 70,000 square feet on two floors. The new facility was designed to accommodate new bike sales, parts and accessories, their line of gifts and apparel, catalog production, warehousing, shipping, and of course, a great shop for building and servicing custom bikes.

Much of the credit for how the store looked on opening day can go to Sherri. She explains, "For a year prior to the opening, the building consumed the majority of my time. I would start the day at the old store with my regular duties and then I would head off to meet Jon Gold, whom we hired as our on-site person for the construction. The two of us were constantly reviewing plans, bids, finances, sourcing materials, and meeting with the architects, vendors, the city as well as the bank. The building became almost overwhelming as it grew in scope. In the two months before it opened, we were usually here until nine p.m. Somehow, in those last few months, I managed to hire an additional twenty-five employees, plan the open house, the parties, the advertising, and even select new apparel to have for sale when the doors opened. The timing couldn't have been more perfect. The Monday after was the last day of our fiscal year. We were exhausted. We were excited. We have never stopped. John never did leave. Having done such a great job with the building, he has stayed on ever since."

As Dublin Mayor Janet Lockhart cut the ribbon in a simple ceremony that Saturday morning, a staff that had recently grown to 70 was ready to greet the customers, who immediately poured through the doors. What they didn't expect was the estimated crowd of 10,000 who showed up over the course of the day. The chief of police, who was attending the ceremony, was helpful in dealing with the overwhelming response. For the first time ever, they closed two of the four lanes of Dublin Boulevard, the street in front of the store, to give the bikes a place to park. Motorcycles were parked as far as the eye could see. The festivities included incredible food that Arlen's good friend Jeff Erb supplied from his Back Forty Texas BBQ restaurant

and four bands that played back to back throughout the day.

While the staff may have felt overwhelmed, they didn't show it as they led the guests around and helped customers. With great excitement, everyone toured the building, spending extra time in the museum. For the first time, Arlen had a fitting area to display some of the many bikes he had built over the years. Fifty of them were beautifully arranged on shiny black granite floor, well lit with spotlights, and surrounded by memorabilia. Visitors could walk through, and between the photos, magazine spreads, trophies, and incredible machines, finally grasp the amazing scope of Arlen's career. The bikes date back to his earliest creations like *Untouchable, VL Chopper,* and the *Peter Max Bike* right up through his most recent bikes, although there are always a couple out for Arlen to ride.

After closing the store at six PM that Saturday, Cory and Kim hosted a party at their

Arlen riding his
Gibson Bike and Cory on
3 Headed Monster,
his *Biker Build-Off*
three-cylinder, Livermore
Hills, California, 2004.

home for the out of town guests and the motorcycle press that went on until one in the morning. On Sunday, the store was open and the celebration continued with more food and another four bands playing all day. After closing that evening, in the large upstairs shop area, Arlen hosted a catered prime rib dinner and Eddie Money performed a concert that had been organized by Sherri as a fundraiser. Only 250 tickets were sold for the event due to a fire department cap on the sales but a lot of money was raised and one hundred percent of the proceeds went to charities. It was the perfect end to an incredible weekend.

The new store brought new challenges and required changes to be made. Arlen says, "I've always had common sense. We never set down on paper what we had to do. We just had things ahead of us that we just knew we had to do. When we started working on the new store, we had to get the bank involved and then we had to have our

first-ever business plan. Before then, we just ran the business and grew it trying all our different ideas on our own."

Cory explains, "This building brings us up another notch, but it does come with a lot more responsibility. It comes with a price. More responsibility, more people, bigger bills, and a bigger nut you have to meet every month. You have to deal with the bank every month. There are cash-flow issues, and you have to satisfy the bank. It requires so much capital to grow."

Cory should know all about the business side of things. By the time they moved into the new store, Cory had been running the show for a number of years. His title was still vice president, but Arlen will be the first to say the title doesn't tell the whole story, "Cory runs it 100 percent. He doesn't even tell me half the stuff. My job is mostly PR. People want to see me and talk to me. I build some bikes for magazine coverage and I get some of the ideas, but Cory does most of the design of the parts anymore. I could walk away today and he could run the whole business without a problem. We're so busy that I just feel guilty if I'm not here."

As for Arlen handling the PR, with his 35 years of experience, he is the pro. For a year prior to the opening of the new store, starting with the annual Sturgis ride, the Travel Channel had been filming a documentary on Arlen. The grand opening, which the crew was waiting for, was filmed as the finale to the one-hour special. The piece also included footage of Arlen and Cory at meetings with Victory and in the Journey Museum exhibition of his bikes that I organized in Rapid City to coincide with Sturgis. This wasn't the first television Arlen had done—he had already appeared many times in both domestic and foreign productions dating back to the early 1990s—but this was a big step. It was a precursor of what was to really start the following year with appearances on the Discovery Channel.

FLASHY KNUCKLE

Arlen did this bike to get a dig in at the antique collectors. He did a magazine spread for *Big Twin* with Beau Pacheco in which the opening spread was a perfect bone stock 1941 Knucklehead that Arlen owned. The following pages were illustrated with this bike to suggest Arlen took a perfect antique and reworked it, something the collectors would loath and a great April Fools' prank. The bike shown was actually built from an old 74-inch Knuckle motor, tranny, and frame Arlen had around the shop along with some spare parts. A Paucho Springer was used in lieu of an original, which Arlen didn't have. Basically, the bike was just assembled, cleaned up, chromed, and painted. Not a typical Ness custom, but is there such a beast?

OHC SPORTSTER

Arlen took a Ness Dyna rubber-mount frame for Big Twins and converted it for this one-of-a-kind 1,200-cc Sportster. Using the proprietary Pete Ardema OHC technology that he and Arlen had used before on the bigger engines, Team Ness reconfigured the stock motor. The sport bike styling suggests perform-ance, reiterated with a racy rear section, back-mounted foot pegs, and the Steve Farone paint scheme. Bob Munroe hand fabricated the aluminum gas tank, rear section, and front fender. Bob also made the pipes, which are routed so they exit high under each side of the rear fender, like road race bikes. To ensure power stopping, a 15-inch brake rotor with a six-piston caliper is mounted on the back wheel, and

dual 13-inch rotors with six-piston calipers are used up front. Arlen made adjustable sliders on the front end so the height of the bike can be modified. He likes the looks of *OHC Sportster* enough to keep it on display in his own office when it is not out on tour or being ridden.

SILVER STREAK

Arlen recalled a silver bike he had built and sold twenty-five years ago when he built *Silver Streak*. He had always liked the simple, elegant look of that first silver bike and decided it would look even better with the latest technologies. He started with a standard Y2K Chopper frame with a five-inch stretch, 38-degree rake and eight-inch rise of the front down tubes. An S&S 111-inch Evo motor was mounted with a five-speed transmission and dressed up with Ness chromed accessories like the rocker covers, cam cover, air cleaner, and tranny

cover. In fact, everything on the bike came out of the Ness catalog right to the Ness wheels and Avon rubber. To complete the plain conservative look he was going for, Arlen bead blasted the wheels, powder-coated the frame silver, and had Jeff McCann do a stylish paint job. Built as a rider, Arlen rode *Silver Streak* to the Frog Jumps and locally around California for some time.

Y2K VICTORY DIGGER

Arlen chose to modify a Ness Y2K Dyna frame to accept the uniconstructed stock 92-inch balanced-shaft Victory motor and transmission for this digger-style bike. Team Ness polished the motor in-house and then sent it out for diamond cutting. As with all Victories, it uses a right-side drive that adds to the smooth, easy riding of this bike. The tank and fenders are stock Ness offerings, as are most of the parts on the bike. Because the oil is integrated into the motor with a wet-sump oil pan, the battery took its place under the seat. Bob Munroe made the exhaust pipes and covers with a jagged appearance to complement the

Steve Farone paint job. German Speed Point wheels were used with dual large-diameter perimeter front brakes and a single perimeter rear brake. A recently introduced wide Avon 250 was used on the rear, which is why Avon used this bike in some of its advertising. Arlen also went with his new flat triple clamps that he has used on many bikes since. He has pointed out that he is not the only one that likes this look; they appeared on stock Harley V-Rods in 2005. Arlen rode this bike around Sturgis when it wasn't on display in Victory stores in 2002. It demonstrates that a full-on Victory custom can be made from readily available parts.

GREEN HORNET

This recent custom by Arlen is powered by a 107-inch S&S motor. To lower the seat height of the Ness Y2K Softail frame, the oil tank was removed from under the seat. Bob Munroe gave it a new location by hand fabricating a combination gas tank-oil tank, leaving just a small cover under the seat to conceal the battery. The Ness Slasher pipes work well with the elongated style the bike takes on from the stock Ness tail-dragger fenders and the five-inch front stretch and 38-degree rake of the frame. Standard Ness wheels include a 21-inch front and 18-inch rear with a wide Avon 250. Brakes, rotors, and accessories throughout the bike are also from the Ness catalog. Arlen likes this style of bike and looks at the building of this one as an exercise in how to make a Softail look long and low.

Helicopter with
Biker Build-Off crew
films Arlen and friends,
Puerto Rico, 2004.

BIKER BUILD-OFF
AND THE FUTURE

Carl Brouhard's sketch for the *Top Banana* build, 2004.

ARLEN has earned many accolades throughout his career, such as when he was the first custom motorcycle fabricator to be named Builder of the Year at the Oakland Roadster Show. He went on to be inducted into both the Sturgis Motorcycle Museum and Hall of Fame and the National Motorcycle Museum and Hall of Fame in Anamosa, Iowa. Several lifetime achievement awards have been bestowed upon him, and he is repeatedly acknowledged by the industry for his contributions to motorcycling.

A recent experience particularly stands out. "CCI brought a number of the people I have known and worked with out to California," Arlen says. "Donnie, Dave, Barry, Grady, my whole family were there. They even

brought Fred Kodlin all the way from Germany. It was kind of like a roast. They made a film from old TV footage and photographs, like the story of my life, and showed it to everyone. There were probably a couple thousand people there. The whole thing was a surprise to me. They said they were going to give me a dealer award to make sure I would show up. Then they brought me on stage and did all that. It was a little embarrassing and very flattering." The awards, the magazine articles, the books, the shows: all have helped build Arlen's name with bikers, with customers, and in the industry. Yet nothing in all his experience can compare to what Arlen was about to encounter with the Discovery Channel's *Biker Build-Offs*.

Arlen explains, "Cory and I were approached about doing a *Biker Build-Off,* but we weren't too excited about it. Especially going against guys like Billy Lane and Indian Larry. It seemed people were more into a completely different kind of motorcycle than we were building. Then a friend of mine, Mike Smith, came up with the idea that we do a build-off against each other. Now that's a real win-win deal. Mike told Hugh King, the *Biker Build-Off* producer, who then called us excited about the idea. From that point, we only had

Arlen working with lead fabricator Jeff Borders, Dublin, California, 2005.

two or three weeks before we had to start the build. That wasn't a whole lot of planning time. We ended up using a lot of parts that we had here at the store.

"We were already filming, thinking we would ride down to L.A., when I got an idea. The finale was scheduled for January when it's cold and ugly out here, so I thought it would be better to go to Hawaii. Hugh agreed, so that's where we went. Everything worked out perfect, getting the bikes to Kona, riding them around the island. Then after the 600-mile ride there, we shipped the bikes to Honolulu for another ride and an event at the Hard Rock Café. The clubs and all the people were gracious, friendly, and excited that we were there. More people came on that ride around Oahu than any other ride they had ever had there. At least that's what Discovery said."

According to the ratings, three million people saw that show when it aired on June 22, 2004. Cory beat Arlen, and it didn't make a bit of a difference. The huge server that hosts the Arlen Ness Web site, appropriately named arlenness.com, couldn't handle all the traffic the show generated. People were

coming into the store who had never been in before, more people were placing orders on the Web site, crowds at events seemed to grow around the Ness truck—it definitely helped all aspects of the business. Arlen says, "They play it so many times, it seems likes everyone sees it. Now when I go to the airport to fly somewhere or just go out anywhere, there are many more people coming up to me, especially the young kids."

For the spring 2004 season, Discovery decided to film a *Build-Off* finale in Laughlin, Nevada, during the annual Laughlin River Run. Arlen describes how it worked: "There were ten builders, and together we built a bike in 72 hours. I was unofficially made the supervisor, I guess because of my age and seniority. It came out great and we made a group decision to give the bike to Hugh King for all the help he has given us."

Not long after Laughlin, when plans were being put together for the fall season, the phone rang again in Arlen's

Arlen fitting lines on *Top Banana*, Dublin, California, 2004.

Arlen working on the final assembly of *Top Banana,* Dublin, California, 2004.

office. This time around, Arlen and Cory were asked to build-off against different builders. "Hugh didn't tell us whom we were going against until just before we had to start the builds," Arlen says. "I wasn't very concerned about who my opponent was going to be, because I knew winning didn't really matter that much after doing the first show. Whether you win or lose, you still get so much PR. I also realized that winning really depends on where the event is or what the crowd is like. Then this time, I had more time to think about what I wanted to build, so I knew I was going to build something a little more special."

Arlen thought he would be pitted against someone like Eddie Trotta, who has also been around for a long time. He thought contrasting Northern California with south Florida could make for good television, but what was finally proposed came as a bit of a surprise. Arlen was to go against a relatively new California builder, Roland Sands, who turned 30 just prior to the build-off. Roland's parents, Perry and Nancy Sands, had founded Performance Machine the same year Arlen moved into his first shop. A great builder, Roland had been

raised in the business just like Cory. His innovative, edgy bikes have a huge appeal with young bikers. Now here was a match full of contrasts. Arlen wondered if it was still a "win-win" situation. If the young builder won, what would this do for Arlen's reputation? If the young builder lost, well then Roland still has 35 years to catch up.

Arlen was up to the challenge. I spent a lot of time with him during the building process and enjoyed seeing the excitement and activity. The creative juices were flowing, and he pulled out all the stops. He actually seemed to glow as he worked. This must have been what it was like when Arlen was working on *Untouchable* or *Two Bad.* The bike came together like I've never seen a bike come together. Everything fit. Everything was ready on or ahead of schedule. Arlen still came into work a bit late and left early. The years of experience showed in every detail. *Top Banana,* as the bike was called, was ready to start up as 50 people looked on. Jeff Borders, Arlen's lead fabricator; other employees; close friends; and the entire Ness family was there. Arlen's brother, Kevin, was

there too, not only as family, but as an employee. A couple of months earlier, Kevin began working for Arlen again, after all those years. Danny Gray, Dick DeBenedictis, Jeff McCann, and Mun were there, too, just as they had been from the beginning, and they worked on this bike as well. The team all wore tuxedoes for the occasion. When they started the bike, everyone toasted the occasion with Dom Perignon. The shared pride in the room was overwhelming.

The party was a great success, but it wasn't the end. There was the big trip ahead. Puerto Rico was selected for the ride, which meant getting the semi full of bikes to the East Coast, on a boat, and through customs before anything could happen. Despite many trials and tribulations, the trip was a fun and fantastic experience. The roads were bumpier than expected, but Arlen handled the long supercharged rigid like the pro he is. Many of

Arlen's friends also came to the island with their bikes just to show their support.

By the end of the day Saturday, they were ready to announce the winner. Hugh King called Arlen and Roland up on the stage in front of the thousands of riders attending Puerto Rico Bike Weekend. After a brief intro-duction, Hugh announced the winner. It was Arlen. Without missing a beat, Roland reached over, shook Arlen's hand, and gave him a huge hug. In this respectful manner, Roland accepted his loss. Arlen, a man of few words, didn't say much more than "Thanks" when he was handed the microphone.

Arlen's recognition goes beyond the motorcycle world. Models of his bikes are sold in Wal-Mart, his T-shirts are available in stores outside the motorcycle industry, and his bikes have been in many exhibitions, including the Guggenheim Museum's "Art of the Motorcycle" exhibit when it traveled to Las

Arlen on stage with Roland Sands and Hugh King after winning his *Biker Build-Off*, Puerto Rico, 2004

Arlen riding with Roland Sands during the filming of their *Biker Build-Off* in Puerto Rico, 2004.

Arlen and Bev right after winning the *Biker Build-Off* with *Top Banana*, Puerto Rico, 2005.

Vegas. So many of the people who now come up to Arlen say they don't ride but they love his bikes and want to say hello. He especially gets a kick when young kids and little old ladies come up and shake his hand, as they often do.

At 65, Arlen still takes good care of himself. For over 15 years, he ran three to four miles a day, but that ended with his broken leg in 1993. Now, he prefers brisk walks with Bev or, if the weather is bad, an hour on the treadmill. He likes to stay in shape. He always enjoyed his vodka martinis straight up, but as I finished writing this book, Arlen told me he decided to stop drinking for a while. He said, "It drags you down and makes you less perky." That typical Arlen Ness: full of surprises!

Arlen drives to work in whichever car he feels like driving. He says, "I have a few fast cars because I like them as well as I like motorcycles. If there's time, I love to take one to Tahoe with Bev. We take the mountain route just because its fun." Fun is still at the heart of Arlen's young spirit. He seems to have fun with everything he does, and with the many toys he has amassed, like the red

Lamborghini Diablo that he purchased recently. He has earned these pleasures, like he's earned the right to go to work when he wants, drive the car he wants, and travel where he wants. Arlen says, "I always watched my money and saved. I liked nice things, but I wouldn't buy something unless I could afford it. I was conservative and always paid my bills." Yet despite where he is now, Arlen still wants to work. He continues, "As long as my health holds up and I enjoy it, I'll keep working. I still work six or seven days a week. I may go in a little bit later or if I don't want to go in, I won't, but it's still fun."

Arlen Ness Enterprises, Inc., is on the move, and moving in the only direction it understands: forward. Cory is clearly running the organization. Like Arlen years before, he has learned how to juggle business duties, public appearances, time to pursue his own bike builds, and family life. With the growth of the business and the way the industry has developed, this could be more demanding than it was on Arlen 35 years ago. In addition to the daily running of the business, Cory has participated in two *Biker Build-Offs* (he won both), was one of the builders on the Hard Rock Roadhouse tour, built a bike for the S&S 145 Tribute project along with several magazine cover bikes, and has continued to work with Victory on his own signature-series bikes.

Even though Cory has developed his own reputation, he still stands behind the "A" that has come to represent the family business, just as he stands behind Arlen. He declares, "My dad doesn't have anything to prove. He didn't self-proclaim himself the 'King' or 'Godfather' of custom motorcycles. He's just stuck with it all these years, and he's been able to keep going."

Cory understands that it's not just the ideas and creative spirit that have brought such success. Determination and commitment have driven Arlen every step of the way. Cory seems to have inherited similar forces, and he wonders if it will continue. "When the third generation comes of age, it could be great or it could be a pain in the ass. Who knows? Sometimes family businesses don't work out." Zach, Cory's son and Arlen's oldest grandchild, shows incredible interest. He has worked at the store and has built his own ground-up customs while still in high school. His brother Max is a lot younger but like any young boy in America today, he loves motorcycles. He already knows what it is like to be in the public eye, having been on television with Arlen's and Cory's *Biker Build-Offs.* Chances are good he will follow in his brother's footsteps.

While Sherri never built a custom bike, she still hopes to get her motorcycle license "some day." She has always been interested in motorcycles, her dad's work, and the family business. Through her daily involvement since 1991, she has a much deeper understanding of this male-dominated industry. She says, "Right now, with the popularity of all the motorcycle TV shows, doors are being opened for boys and particularly for girls. My own daughters, Taylor and Samantha, watch what's on TV, see what grandpa is doing, and have opinions of their own. They feel a part of it and know there may be opportunities for them down the road. Maybe Taylor will start

by building a bike with my husband. She has expressed the interest. For now, she enjoys working in the store. Samantha is just enjoying being nine. Wherever they end up, I would love for both of them to learn how to ride street bikes." They are off to a good start. Both of them already ride dirt bikes and

Arlen and *Top Banana,* Dublin, California, 2004.

Arlen toasts his
Team Ness with Dom
Perignon after starting
the *Biker Build-Off* bike
Top Banana ,
Dublin, California, 2004.

Sherri's husband, Craig Foxworthy, is an accomplished builder and painter in his own right. Motorcycling is coming at them from both parents.

In reflecting on his career and custom bike building, Arlen says, "For a lot of years, I was on top of the pile. Now that there are so many builders doing great work, we all share the limelight, but there is plenty to go around. I hope we can stay in it and keep building our brand, which is really the Ness name. Maybe the family will stay in it if they're

interested. We'll see who wants to. I'd be proud if all four grandchildren wanted to work here and eventually run it. Then it can just keep on going."

The "it" that Arlen refers to is, of course, the incredible business he has built, which some people think of more as an empire. It is also the Ness name and that indelible "A" logo that's been used over and over for so many years. I believe it's more than wishful thinking by this man that I call the "King." His "A" will reign for years to come.

GIBSON BIKE

The *Gibson Bike* was built for a Gibson guitar project called the "Kings of Customs," which also included old friends Donnie Smith and Dave Perewitz. Each builder was given a guitar to paint similar to a guitar-themed bike they were to build. Arlen chose one of his Y2K rubber-mount chopper frames, which has an eight-inch rise added to the front down tubes, a five-inch stretch in the top bar, and a 38-degree rake at the neck. The long Ness front end connects to 4-degree raked flat Ness triple trees.

The Ness billet wheels are diamond cut and powder-coated blue and are mounted with Avon rubber, a 250x18 on the rear and a wide 21-inch up front. The 124-inch motor is from S&S, as is the carburetor. Arlen modified a standard Ness tank with sheet metal to cosmetically close the gap between the top bar and the motor. Dick DeBenedictis did a great job painting the bike and the guitar. He used arcs that mimic shapes in the bike itself like the curved back of the frame, the Ness Slasher pipes, the air cleaner, and fenders.

HAWAII BUILD-OFF BIKE

With little advance notice and a very tight schedule imposed by the Discovery Channel, Arlen's *Hawaii Build-Off Bike* was built in 30 days. He started with the same Y2K frame, gas tank, and front end he had just used on the Gibson bike and then chose the large 145-inch S&S motor that he helped introduce less than a year before when he was part of S&S's 145-inch tribute project. He also used the same special-purpose transmission that was designed and manufactured for him to use in the 145-inch project by Baker Drivetrain. It is a five-speed dual drive with pulleys out both sides that are particularly useful with big horsepower motors. The dual rear belts turn the 18-inch wheel with Arlen's signature "A" cut right

into it. The Avon 300 mounted on it, despite being the largest tire on the market at the time, fits perfectly in the tightly wrapped cutaway fender that Arlen made himself. He also hand fabricated the front fender and one-off pipes. A long Ness front end was mounted to Arlen's flat-raked triple trees. Arlen went as loud as he could, painting the base and flames himself, knowing this

would be a "TV bike." To make the tight deadline, final graphics and striping were done by two painters, Steve Farone and Jon Kosmoski, who founded House of Kolor paints. Arlen has only good things to say about the trip to Hawaii with the bike. While technically he lost to Cory, it was a "win-win" opportunity that worked out for everyone.

TOP BANANA

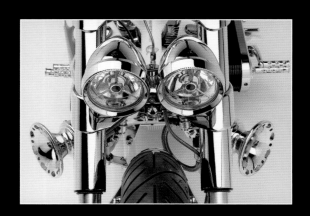

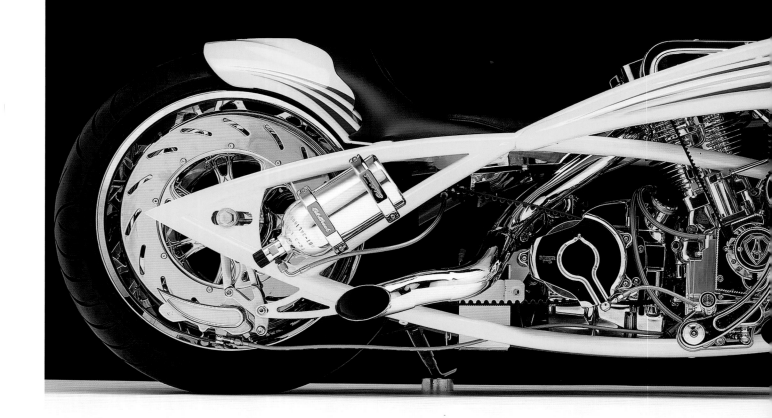

TOP BANANA

Arlen recently said it had been a long time since he had built a serious bike, "I've just been building fun bikes and choppers." He definitely went all out on this project, which he was only given ten days to complete. Starting with the one-off frame that envelopes the 145-inch S&S motor, he and Bob Munroe bent PVC tubing to determine the correct radius that could work throughout the bike. The engine was modified to an OHC design and a super-charger with two S&S carbs was added to maximize performance. To keep the bike long and low, there are two top bars that split apart with the gas tanks, so the engine can come right up between them. Wheels are like the *Hawaii Build-Off Bike*, 21-inch front and 18-inch rear, with Arlen's signature "A" cut into them. The large 300 Avon is turned with dual rear belts coming off of a special Baker transmission. Dual one-off front perimeter brakes were used with dual rear six-piston calipers on the rear. Danny Gray's two-part seat was cushier than it

looked, with springs that fit in a deep
seat pan to help soften the rigid ride. Arlen
applied the base paint, and Dick
DeBenedictis painted the abundant
graphics on the inside and outside of the
long split tanks. The *Build-Off* ride with
Roland Sands took place in Puerto Rico in
December 2004. It seemed appropriate that
Arlen and his *Top Banana* won, which
seemed to recognize not just a great bike
but his many years of experience and
longstanding relationships with artisans like
Bob, Danny, and Dick, who have been with
Arlen since the beginning.

NESS SIGNATURE VICTORY KINGPIN

This bike is a production bike off the Victory Motorcycles assembly line, but it has a lot of Arlen in it. It is the result of working with Victory since he and Cory signed a formal agreement in 2001. Acting as design consultants, they have given styling input ever since. Their biggest influence was probably with the Victory Vegas, which were released in 2003, and with which he also did a red-and-black Signature Series bike. Being a large motorcycle manufacturer, there are only certain aspects of the design they could affect, such as the longer fenders on all Kingpin models. This represented a change from the earlier stubby fenders, and the

shape of the tank, which is the same as the Vegas that Arlen and Cory helped design. For this Signature Series bike, Arlen also put together the paint scheme and dressed the bike with an assortment of Ness parts, such as the 18-inch front and rear billet wheels, handlebars, mirrors, grips, and pegs. Cory came out with his own

Signature Series bike in 2004 as well. At the core of these bikes are stock 92-inch Victory motors unit constructed with five-speed transmissions. Arlen believes strongly enough in Victory, their bikes, and their engines that he is happy to have his signature on the side cover of each bike along with his trademarked "A."

JET BIKE

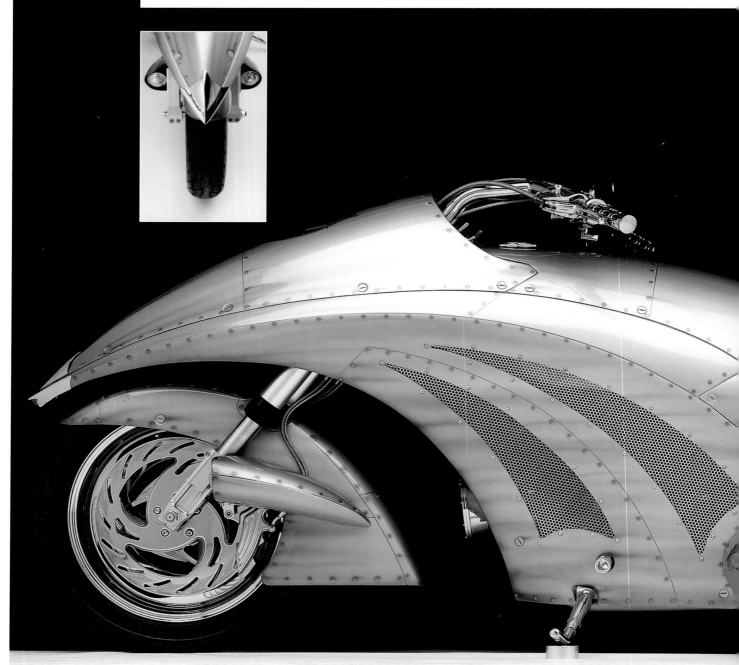

Arlen's interest in building *Jet Bike* dates back several years to when Jay Leno rode one into an L.A. event and up to the Ness truck. Arlen thought, "This is cool. I've got to have one," but after hearing it cost over $250,000, he decided to build his own. Barry Cooney found a jet engine, like one used in helicopters, for sale on the Internet. Knowing it would work, Arlen purchased the turbine and set out to fit it into an old Ness frame that he cut up.

With a shaft coming out the end and no transmission required, Arlen used a single chain to deliver power to the rear wheel. A clutch was installed to disengage the engine as needed. Because two 12-volt marine batteries are necessary to generate the 24-volts needed to start the turbine, Arlen decided to mount an electric motor with friction drive in front of the rear wheel so he could easily move the bike in a situation where he didn't want to start the

JET FUEL ONLY

AFTER · AUX · TURBINE · MAIN
POWER · OVERIDE · POWER

mach ness

CAUTION
EXHAUST BLAST

jet. To stop the bike quickly, two six-piston caliper brakes with 13-inch rotors were mounted on the front and one on the back. All other working parts came from the Ness catalog. Arlen's goal for the bike was to create a long and low look that keeps the jet theme compared to other jet-powered bikes that have been built as sport bikes. He loves the sound but doesn't think the engine is appealing enough to expose. To achieve this, Bob Munroe hand fabricated an all aluminum body that looks like the body of a jet and Carl Brouhard painted faux graphics that are so detailed, it seems rust has built up behind the painted rivets from so many flight hours! With afterburner flames shooting back ten feet, Arlen is ready to move forward, but who can guess what his next creation will be.

INDEX